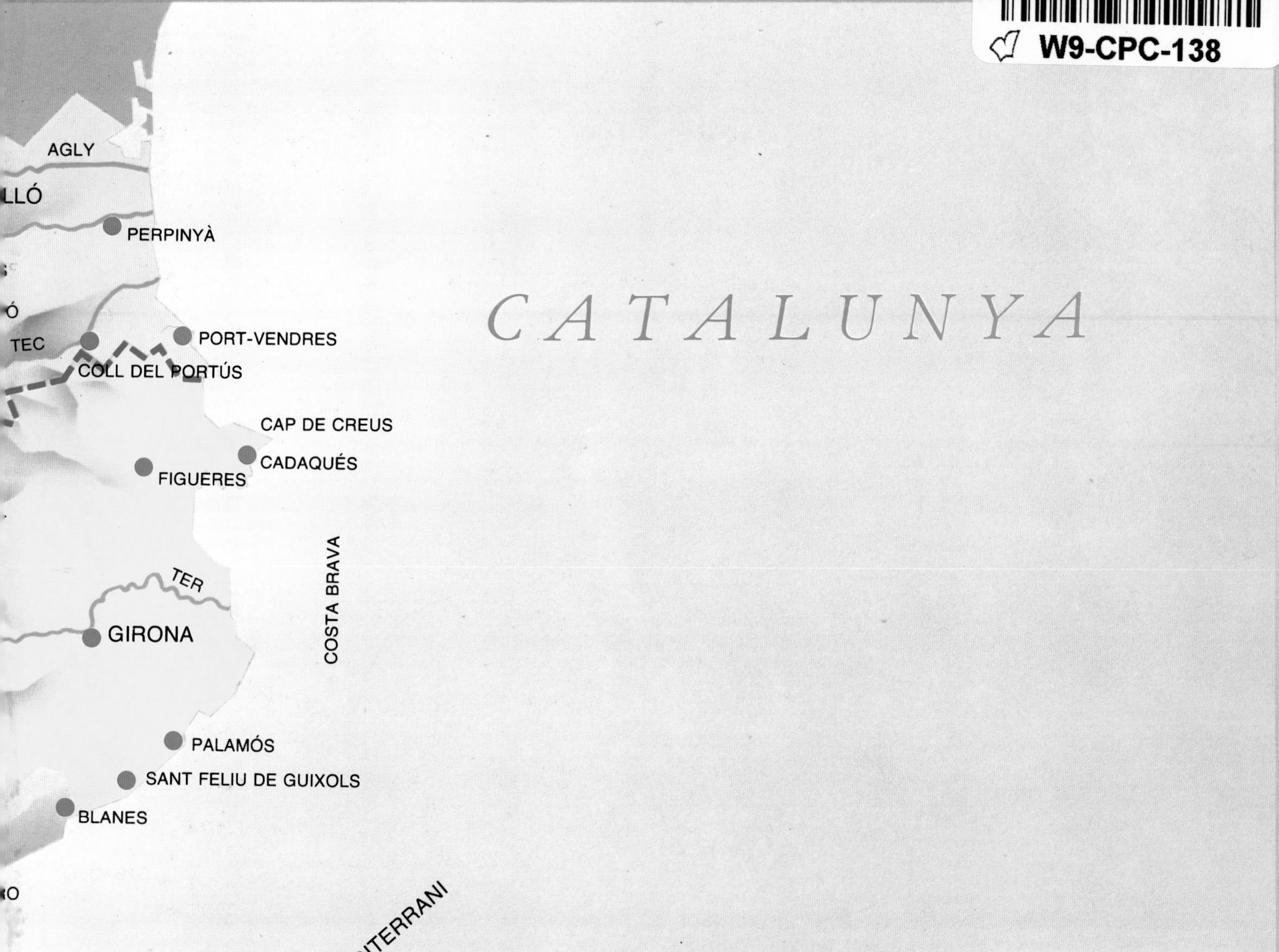

AGLY

LLÓ

PERPINYÀ

Ó

TEC

PORT-VENDRES

COLL DEL PORTÚS

CAP DE CREUS

CADAQUÉS

FIGUERES

TER

COSTA BRAVA

GIRONA

PALAMÓS

SANT FELIU DE GUIXOLS

BLANES

O

CATALUNYA

MAR MEDITERRANI

SEEING CATALONIA

Text by
Josep Pla
and Christian Sarramon

Illustrated by
Christian Sarramon

Ediciones Destino

© EDICIONES DESTINO, S.A.
Consell de Cent, 425. 08009 Barcelona
Translated by Verònica Teixidor de Ventós
First published in English: August 1983
Second published in English: May 1985
Third published in English: April 1988
Fourth published in English: November 1993
ISBN: 84-233-1258-5
D.L.: B. 38.374-1993
Printed in Spain by
Indústries Gráfiques Immer, S.A.
Torrent dels Murris, 17. La Garriga (Barcelona)

Catalonia and Roussillon

**Tarragona, Roman columns and cypress trees, symbols of the latin world.
Photo: Ramon Dimas.**

Catalonia and Roussillon are situated on either side of the eastern range of the Pyrenees. They were two countries which were united harmoniously until the signing of the Treaty of the Pyrenees, a little over three hundred years ago. During that long period of union there was only one problem which was the will of the King of Catalonia, James I the Conqueror, who bequeathed Catalonia and Aragon to one of his sons, and Majorca and Roussillon to the other. I have a great respect for James I the Conqueror but not for the author of this will, quite the reverse. He was a king who one supposes had an idea of what a state and a country are yet he caused a civil war. That was disastrous. Shall we ever have a real history of our country? Patriotism, especially historic patriotism, is tiring.

Catalonia and Roussillon, including the Vallespir, the Conflent and all the area situated between the Albera and the Corbières, formed a unit. They were part of the Roman Empire. The Roman Empire came to our country as a consequence of taking over Empúries,[1] a small Greek settlement of purely commercial origin. Miletus in Asia Minor had more than eighty commercial establishments by the end of the second Greek millennium and notably Massilia, the actual Marseilles, which is always cited as having contributed to the conception of Empúries. Was it not itself a creation of Miletus? The old Massilia is surrounded by Greek settlements. The Roman legions absorbed Empúries easily, as one would gobble a peach in summer. No difficulties. To the north of the Greek settlement, which has been mostly excavated now, they are excavating Roman remains, most of which have not been studied. To the south of it there is a Roman wall standing and the site of the building which must have been for shows of some sort and which was protected by the wall from the tramontana wind. In the last few years they have excavated some Roman living spaces with some results. It is a pity though that they have not yet erected in the Greek establishment a stone or something stating that it was here that the romanization of the Iberian Peninsula began.

1. Place-names have been left in Catalan except when a translated form is well known in English (e.g. Catalonia, Roussillon).

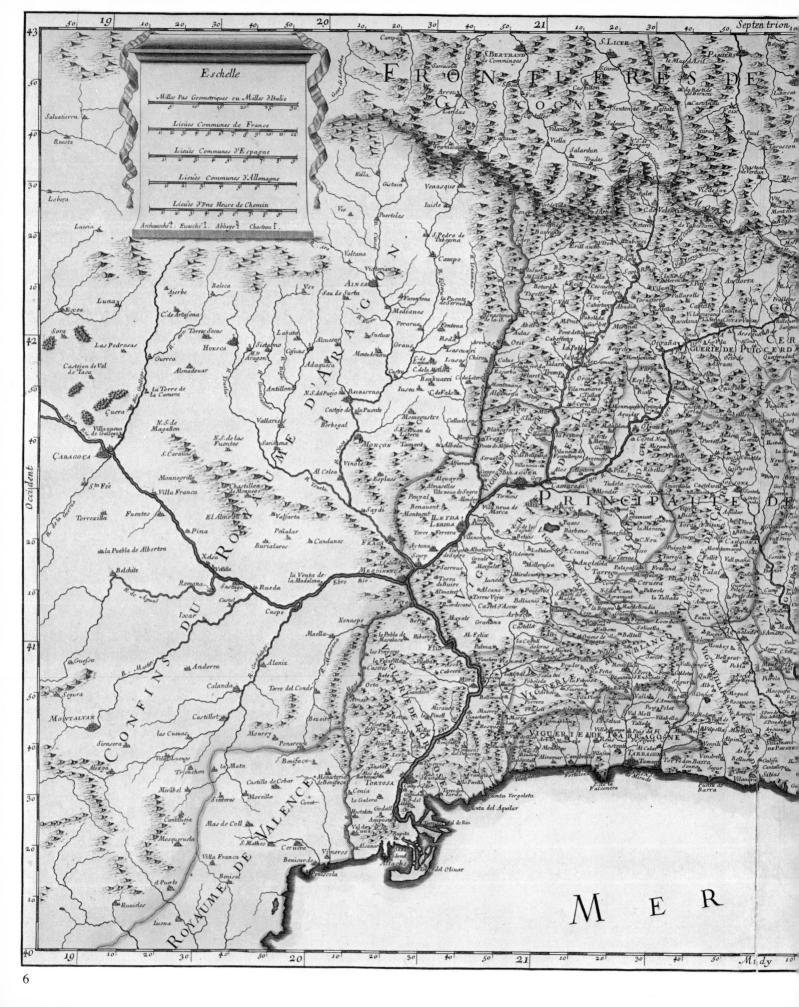

French map of
Catalonia,
dated 1674,
shortly after the
Treaty of the
Pyrenees.

7

Barcelona, the Rambla, the Passeig de Gràcia and the Park of the Ciutadella, at the beginning of the century, the time of the Eixample urban plan.

31. BARCELONA — Paseo de Gracia
L. Roisin, fot. Barcelona

98   BARCELONA — El Parque. — La Cascada. — LL.

8

It was the Roman Empire, with the ups and downs normal to any military campaign, which dominated the Peninsula. The Peninsula was divided in three provinces Tarraconense, Lusitania and Betica. The Roman capital of our country was Tarragona. In Languedoc it was Narbonne. The very north of the Peninsula they didn't name because it was the most difficult to conquer. Anyway this is how our country started being romanized. The philologists say that Latin started to be corrupted sooner in the areas outside Rome than in Italy itself, because in Italy Latin was defended by the Church. The tenacity of the church in maintaining Latin was admirable. The corruption of Latin gave rise to the vulgar languages, Catalan in our case. In Italy this corruption occurred a few centuries later. This is how our language gradually developed. Basically we retained the Roman Law that even today is supplementary. Our way of being was nothing other than that of Roman colonials who became Roman citizens. The large or small number of people who lived in these circumstances were Roman citizens. What else could you ask for? The people who lived around here were Roman citizens. Could you ask for more? I think that we were very lucky. We became part of the only civilization existing. The people with curiosity will soon realize that. Those who have none will learn nothing, as always.

Girls of the Roussillon bourgeoisie in traditional dresses, around 1900.

The Greeks of Empúries made some paths. They were people dedicated to commerce, to buying and selling. They bought and sold to the prehistoric people of the country. The Romans built important roads which have survived to this day. Rome had to be fed. The Romans bought lots of things from this country, particularly meat from the Pyrenees which was then sent to Rome. The great capital had to be maintained. It seems that the Tarraconense region never experienced any problems. The system of romanization in our country lasted for centuries. Even today in Tarragona, in Barcelona and in lots of other places one can find important Roman remains. There was the conversion to the triumphant religion, Catholicism. I don't think there was any difficulty. Tarragona became the capital of our catholicism. Then the northern invaders arrived, the northern Barbarians, Goths and Visigoths etc. And it was extraordinary. For some reason, maybe because it

108 BARCELONA. — El parque de Güell. — El pont de Dalt. — LL.

Barcelona. To the left: the top bridge of
the Park Güell. To the right: La Sagrada
Família, unfinished work of
Antoni Gaudí.

Drawing of Gaudí by Ricardo Opisso.

was easier, because of laziness, these people became Roman
very easily. They mixed up. The Roman world was maybe
destroyed, but up to a point only. They integrated; they felt at
home. The country got on reasonably well, above all on
account of the strength provided by the order of St. Benedict
which, with the introduction of the feudal system, gave the
country a new appearance.

The greatest changes were produced later with the appearance of the invading Moors from the south. These people
were much more difficult to break up. They passed through
Old Catalonia like a bullet both on the way to invade France
and on the way back when they returned defeated. They left no
traces of their passage. It was not the same in New Catalonia,
and the Catalan countries of Valencia and Majorca, where
they stayed for centuries. For the history of this country this
element is very important because it was the fight against these
people and their invasions that after all created the idea of
unity in the peninsula. It was the fight against the Moors which
after all created a unity which was basically religious, catholic,
apostolic and Roman. It was a fight which lasted for centuries,
excessively long and sometimes ridiculous. The chief of Cova-

donga did the same as the Catalan count-kings, that is he fought against the Moors. James the Conqueror took over the kingdom of Valencia and Majorca in the same way that the Catholic Kings took over Granada, and the domination thus ended. The operation lasted many years but in the end it was resolved. This long operation, though, gave rise to relations between the political leaders of the peninsula. It is on account of this that many historians have deduced the religious unity of Spain. This is important. Still this belongs to the past but to overcome the things of the past is not easy.

I must ask my readers forgiveness for the limitations of this paper. It is too short. To write the history of this country in a few pages is perhaps excessive. I hope that the reader will be kind enough to look through a history book to see what I have hardly been able to say.

It is not that I don't like things short and clear. Everything I write is like that. But a few pages in which to provide a summary of our history may be a bit too much. But of course in these times this is the reality. Once the authentic Catalan monarchy had been destroyed, unfortunately destroyed and to the detriment of the religious unity which had been established by the war against the Moors, this country was ruled by another dynasty, the Trastamara family, who produced an incredible, historical chaos. I am not going to refer to these facts because they have been fully studied and are well known. Really they are used as an excuse for polemical debate and it is better not to add to this, as our bad luck in history is real enough. Let us not try and inflame what is already inflamed in this century, which is one of the most sinister and difficult ones which our continent has experienced. After all we must provide some of the permanent bases of the country. I am referring now to the romanization of the country and to our way of talking and of being. I am sorry but I shall make a reference to Socrates. This incredible person believed that in the human thought there are only two ideas, the precepts and opinions. The precepts are the human realities which have been studied, observed, formulated, about which everything is known and which are based on experience. Of opinions he never took any notice. He considered that they were the phenomena of ignorance, pure human primitiveness. Now, we can put a man like Socrates in the hands of Plato, a superb writer, perhaps the best of the classics, and we shall see the greatness of the thirty six dialogues which are still alive and shall always be.

Barcelona, the port and the Castle of Montjuïc at the beginning of the century.

Catalonia is surrounded by what have been called the Catalan countries. It is certain that the country most attached to Catalonia has been Roussillon. Everything makes us suppose that this link is very ancient. The Roussillon is a marvellous country, firstly because it is surrounded by the Albera, the Corbières, the sea and the mountains of Cerdagne, which are French. It is dominated by the peak of Canigó. It is a very rich country, well cultivated as it benefits from the abundance of the waters of the Canigó. Water is the richness of earth, and that from the Canigó, channelled by the Catalan monarchy, never fails. The poet Verdaguer wrote that the Roussillon is an instrument with three strings: the Tec, the Tet and the Aglí which are its water courses. The link between

these two countries can be dated back to Charlemagne and his successors who created the "Spanish March". Charlemagne was the greatest political and religious leader of his time. All the formative influences on Old Catalonia, are Languedocian. There is no doubt of this in the case of the county basis of government. The Catalan monarchy originated in Carcassonne. Catalonia and Roussillon have always felt an attraction to the north. That they had illusions of this kind there is no doubt. Catalonia and Roussillon possessed lots of Languedocian territory.

What were their aims? Nobody knows as everything remains to be studied. Something fabulous no doubt. There was no doubt that there was a degree of madness in the county of Toulouse-Languedoc. And the Albigensians? It was a strange situation. The destruction of the religious unity was a vast affair. The French policy of langue d'oil, won with the help of the English adventurer, Simon de Montfort. Everything was destroyed at the battle of Muret. It was the father of James the Conqueror (born in Montpellier) who lost. All illusions disappeared, shattered by this defeat. Years went by and now it is over three centuries since the signing of the Treaty of the Pyrenees by which France reached the Pyrenean mountain

Sardanas at the port, nets on the beach, Corpus procession, familiar images of a disappearing society. Anonymous photos of Estartit taken between 1910 and 1930.

chain, which is called its natural frontier. Part of Cerdagne and all of Roussillon became French territory. Important losses. The annexation was perhaps a bit difficult and complex but time consolidates everything. The new situation meant something very different. Roussillon and Catalonia which had lived as permanent and positive neighbours for so long became separated and profoundly so in many aspects. In the case of Roussillon there was a total indifference to this and in the case of Catalonia, ignorance.

Roussillon, abbey of Sant Martí del Canigó, before its restoration.

In the last century Catalonia was divided into provinces, on the model of French "départements". There were four: Barcelona, Girona, Lleida and Tarragona. In the cases of the French départements prefectures and sometimes subprefectures were established. In the Peninsula only civil governments were set up. In previous periods Catalonia had had other administrative divisions which were not considered. In our historical process the Trastamaras, the Bourbons, the Austrians and the varied régimes of the nineteenth century made important attempts at administrative reform. Those which have lasted longest have been the civil governments. Catalonia's capital, Barcelona, is a "Capitanía General", the fourth in Spain.

From the (strictly historical) point of view Catalonia has had another division. The Old Catalonia and the New. These two areas are separated by the river Llobregat, which reaches the sea very near the Coast of Garraf, and are historically distinct. In the Medieval Ages counties were set up in the Old Catalonia. In the Empordà, which was attached to Roussillon, the county of Empúries was established by the successors of Charlemagne. The Muslim invasions passed through this area on the way to and back from France where they were defeated. They left no imprint. In the Old Catalonia there are no Muslim traces. The elimination of the Moors in the New Catalonia, however, took longer and was more complicated. From the fact originated the essence of the ideal of the Medieval Peninsula: its religious unity, catholic, apostolic and Roman. When during that struggle the Catalans reached

Siurana, the reigning count-king created Poblet and installed Cistercian monks from Languedoc. Montserrat, a benedictine abbey, owed its origins to Carcassonne and the Benedictines imposed the monarchial ideas on the counts of Barcelona who quickly became the most important.

Everything makes one suppose that during centuries this country, lightly inhabited, lived off agriculture and led the most miserable of existences. But Barcelona, a big city, a commercial and maritime centre, provided succour to the rest of the country. Barcelona had a lively port. It created a lot of consulates in the Mediterranean to buy what was needed and sell what there was in excess. Barcelona became the key to the whole area. Sometimes Barcelona appears like a free Italian city, with great dynamism.

Penedès, having a rest during grape picking. Photo: F. Català-Roca.

At the same time as the establishment of the Trastamara dynasty the so called war of the "Remences" started in Old Catalonia. It was the first agrarian uprising against feudalism in this continent, which is to say a lot, and also a long lasting insurrection against the main authority of the country, which was the "Generalitat". The war of the "Remences" has been very well studied by the historian Vicens Vives. Some of the references to the conflict made by Polish and Russians, which Vicens Vives showed me, are insignificant and the products of ignorance. This is a country which has experienced long peaceful phases in its history as well as sudden extremist explosions. Vicens studied not only the war itself but also the document which finished it which was the "Sentencia de Guadalupe", an agreement made by the Catalan king in front of a lot witnesses from this country. It was certainly a good thing. People who say that this country has never done anything good probably exaggerate because there are exceptions. One of them is this "Sentencia de Guadalupe". From the popular point of view this should be well known, but it is not unfortunately the case.

Once the Austrian monarchy, which in general respected the ancient Catalan rights and privileges, was installed, the country accepted it. Barcelona became a tremendous dockyard, as a consequence of the favourable policy of the Habsburgs in the Mediterranean. Charles the Fifth, and Philip II who built the Escorial, represent the highest point of the Castilian Empire. The pillage of Rome by the first, and the Invincible Armada of the second, seem complete acts of madness, impossible to explain. I suppose that there is no doubt about the fact that this country was in favour of the Habsburgs. Things went all right and they got along. In the government of the Habsburgs there was a remarkable madman, the count-duke of Olivares. Doctor Marañón wrote a great book about him which contains a lot of real information. He was the cause of the greatest difficulties which arose between Madrid and Barcelona during this period, a real Castilian invasion, led by the Marquis of Velez. It was a difficult and complicated invasion which has no explanation apart from the despotic and fanatic character of the centralist leader Olivares. A great disaster.

One of the popular representations of the Passion, very common in Catalonia. Photo: Pere Català-Roca.

The exhaustion of the Austrian dynasty produced the War of Spanish Succession between the Habsburgs and the Bourbons. Generally speaking Catalonia and the elements of the Old Confederation were pro Austrian. French diplomacy though won and a new king from the house of Paris appeared, Philip V. The big European powers were the Habsburgs and Bourbons and Catalonia had to pay for its weakness with the publication of the Decree of Nova Planta by which all the old freedoms of Catalonia were abolished. Another big disaster. One of the matters which caused a strong reaction apart from this decree, was the closure of the University of Barcelona and the construction in Cervera de Lleida of a new university. The construction of this incredible building, today as empty as an empty cage, was not as useless as some people claim. Of course it was a conservative and official University, which had excellent professors and students. It was impossible to choose because there was no other choice. The years went by and things became more relaxed. The Bourbon monarchy had a great king, Charles III, who had been king of Naples. It was this man who opened widely the Bourbon gates. This king, who had a good name, merits a real study. It was the continuous madnesses of the last century which started with the Napoleonic invasions and finished in the last civil war, which caused Catalonia to examine its personality. This country had been slowly industrializing with difficulties, but there was need of a stable system to get on ahead and to put a stop to smuggling, specially English smuggling, permitted by the liberal economic system followed in Madrid and sometimes defended by Catalans like Sr. Figuerola and others. It was necessary to create an elementary protective system practised everywhere else to fight the English smuggling which was directed against Catalan industralization, which after all was the only way to feed a town like Barcelona growing all the time. It took a long time to arrange that but in the end the industry of the country succeeded apart form the cork industry which remained marginal and it is for that reason that there are so many factories in the world without real knowledge of the cork.

The compiling of the Civil Code, in great part copied from the Napoleonic Code, established our law and our way of being. The minister Duran i Bas suceeded in the creating of Catalan jurists who had to complete the supplementary study of the Catalan law. Years went by and the commission did nothing. Several more years went by and the Señores Coromines, Faus, Porcioles, Roca Sastre and others managed to get the said agreement approved. When I arrived in Barcelona there was only one library, an anarchist one, not a single museum and all the academic corporations were dead. Maybe the Academy of Good Letters was more alive. Luckily things were changing. The Institute had been created, the Library of Catalonia was starting to collect romanesque paintings, the basis of all later museums. A modern country had started to grow particularly with all the scholarships provided to study abroad in Germany, Brussels and Paris. Politics had taken a more Catalan and Catalanist turn. The intellectual and administrative political group which appeared then has never since had a like. The Mancomunitat was near. The works of its first president, Enric Prat de la Riba, had a profound effect in

The "Xiquets" of Valls build their human castles on days of festivities.
Photo: Ramon Dimas.

all matters: political, cultural and urban. If Prat had lived longer he would have changed Catalonia.

I must make a short and comprehensive reference to the provinces. We are supposing that now there will be a Statute re-establishing the Generalitat in an autonomous form, with more political and administrative powers. We shall see if its powers will be greater or less. Whatever happens some organs of government will continue to function in the old way. In this connection it would be very important to establish two more provinces, Vic in the north, and Tortosa in the south. The capitals of provinces were established on the basis of impressive cathedrals, Barcelona, Tarragona, Girona, Lleida. Meanwhile we should fight with all arms the instinct of destruction which our country has suffered from. In my memory there has occurred the destruction of Ripoll (apart from the gate and the cloister) which was a first class centre, Sant Pere de Roda, Sant Quirze de Colera, Santa Maria de Roses, Sant Feliu de Guíxols (Benedictine cenoby) and so many other things that the list would be unending. The destruction of works of art and of our most authentic traditions should fill us with shame. Destructions have a lot of causes but the principal one is always politics. They have wanted to make a political unity of the Peninsula based on religion and opponents of this aim have responded by destroying everything.

To finish I would only ask Mr. Sarramon, an admirer of Catalonia and Roussillon and an extraordinary photographer, to take the actual photos of the country.

Josep Pla

The Roussillon

The Roussillon is very beautiful, prodigiously so. There are lots of things there. Despite the neglect of its monuments by French neoclacissists and the burning and sacking to which they have been afflicted its archaeological treasures are marvellous. A part of the cloister of St. Miquel de Cuixà is today the "cloisters" of New York. The politics and the famed sensibility of the modern Frenchman showed a complete disdain for the romanesque and the gothic styles, considered as relics of obscurity and fanaticism. They destroyed what they could but not all because they lacked the time.

On the other hand the Roussillon is an earthly paradise. It is the country of tender leaves, of the vine, of fruit. The Ceret cherries, how marvellous they are! Around April the first cherries start to blossom. A cherry tree in flower is one of the most beautiful trees that one can imagine.

Now it is the time to eat twenty or twenty five big, fat and juicy grilled sardines and half a kilo of cherries. This is the menu at this moment of Spring. The cherries vary with the years: sometimes they are incomparable, sometimes they are not quite of the best. The cherry must be hard, the skin has to break at the touch of the teeth, its flesh must be consistent and fresh. In this world, though, there are never two things the same. Everythings is sometimes less, sometimes more. In any case, a basket full of Roussillon cherries, and particularly those of Ceret, has a brightness and a colour one never forgets.

Yes it is certain that to doubt has no sense. The Roussillon possesses a great quantity of water. This abundance comes from the mountain of Canigó. If the Canigó was not an inexhaustible fountain of water the notaries of the country would not count for so much. In sunny countries the water is the condition of the richness of the earth. The plains of the Roussillon are traversed by three rivers, the Tet, the Tec and the Aglí and by many water conducts some of which date from the times of the Catalan kings. Compared to the Roussillon, the Empordà is still in prehistoric times. Almost all the water which traverses it is lost in the sea; the multisecular immobilism has created a type of routine-bound human being, pretentious and believing he knows all, with little capacity in

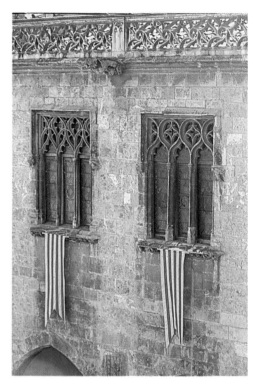

Perpignan, Gothic windows of the Llotja[1] de Mar with the Catalan flag.

1. Llotja: Stock exchange.

20

eliminating his ignorance, and leading a narrow life and making little effort. But without schools how do you expect people to end up! Agriculture is studied like in the old times embroidery was taught to ladies in a nun's school. It is a refined, silly and bookish agriculture which only inspires one desire: to leave the land. If we started to talk about all that we would never finish. The fact is that the Empordà, particularly the high Empordà which is potentially one of the richest counties of our country, is one of the most abandoned, and relatively one of the least productive.

And so I like all aspects of the Roussillon. I am enchanted by Perpignan. I frequent the bookshops, the cafés and the streets. I like the life of Perpignan, the sedentary one and wandering around gazing. I read the papers in the café de la Llotja, which is an old and accredited establishment, with mirrors and with a majority of its customers people who enjoy the good things of this world, sceptic people, arthritic and full of sense. The Llotja de Mar, made with old stone and in gothic style, is in front of me. Next to it is the Town Hall, which is a beautiful building with a porched patio. In it there is the "Venus Mediterrania" by Maillol, which is a perfect, serene and intelligent piece of sculpture. The small quadrangle made by these buildings is the place of rendez-vous not only of the Perpignanais from the immediate vicinity and of the tourists but of all the important Roussillonais. I walk around the narrow streets of the town centre, some of which have wooden arches. I gaze at the shopwindows, sometimes very brilliant. I go in and out of the cathedral which has the defect in my opinion of having the front built with drift-wood from the river and it makes a contrast with the lovely and tranquil square in front.

Of the old wall in the lower part of the city (looking towards France) there only remains the famous Castellet, a brick building of a remarkable crudity of colour which if it had been built with stone would seem more historical. The idea of allowing a stream of water to flow at the base of what were the walls, and which today is the site of the Prefecture, the Grand Hotel and some other important buildings, was a correct one. To that urban stream they have added recently a perimeter of reinforced concrete and some nicely arranged gardens. It is a little stream dressed in its Sunday best and the trees which shade it are quite nice. On top of the bridge over the stream there is the Palmarium, a huge and cold café of monstruous dimensions and it is here that started the growth of the town in the direction of the station. It is traditional to go and view the Canigó from the Palmarium. From the café terrace the views of the mountains are perfect.

J. P.

"The Mediterranean Venus" by Maillol. House of the city of Perpignan.

Detail of the wall of the Castellet, important remains of the walls of Perpignan, today museums of art and of Catalan traditions.

Salses

The Pass of Salses, which links the Roussillon with Lower Languedoc, has always been the strategic key to the north of Catalonia. In the year 218 B. C. Hannibal had to negotiate with the tribes of Gaul to continue on his way to Italy. The Romans made a camp here and in the eight century the Saracens built the first fortification in this strategically crucial pass.

But this impressive fortification which is half buried amongst the vineyards as if it was a sandcastle made by an ingenious child, and which we can see now from the motorway, dates from the fifteenth century.

After the return of Roussillon to Spain, Ferdinand of Aragon, wanting to protect his northern frontiers, arranged for an engineer called Ramirez to build this fortification, designed for a garrison of three thousand men with their horses and reserves. When Richelieu started the conquest of Roussillon, Salses was the occasion of a ferocious fight between Spaniards and French. Finally, in 1642, after the fall of Perpignan, the governor of Salses retreated after having received all the honours of war.

In the Treaty of the Pyrenees in 1659 the "natural frontiers" were pushed back to the Pyrenees, the Roussillon became French and Salses lost for ever its role of sentinel.

Modified by Vauban, who decreased its elegance by decapitating the tower of homage and the torricons, the fortification of Salses still remains a rare example of Spanish architecture of the fifteenth and sixteenth centuries in which a new technique in fortifications developed in accordance with the needs imposed by developments in weaponry.

Aerial view of the castle of Salses (15th C.).

A Land blessed by the gods

Inhabited since the beginning of the human race (the craneums excavated in Tautavel are the oldest found in Europe) and very populated in Roman times of "Ruscino" (now Château-Roussillon), this plain, which took the name of Roussillon, has always excited envy. The reason is that this sunny land, irrigated all the year round by the waters of the Canigó, is one of the richest in France. Agriculture reigns here because everything grows well. And not only on the plain but also in the high valleys of the Vallespir, the Conflent and Cerdanya. With the proximity of a commercial sea, by which means it could export all its products, all this region, dependent on Catalonia from the year one thousand, presented in the Middle Ages a very similar aspect to that of today; a vast garden scattered with rich towns. The fruit trees, the vegetables and also the vineyards, stretching without interruption from the Corbières to the Albera, are the specialities of the agriculture of Roussillon and decorate the countryside according to seasons. From the point of view of the fruit the most important production is that of peaches which ripen between June and September. But also apricots and nectarines have been planted lately. The cherries, the first of which ripen in mid April, come from Ceret. The vegetables, often grown amongst the fruit trees or cultivated in greenhouses, give about three harvests annually on the same bit of land.

The vineyards produce sweet wines of great tradition (Banyuls, Mauri, Ribesaltes, well known for its muscatel). Aperitif wines, vermouths and all sorts of sweet wines, to which the heat, the quality of the soil and the privileged geographical situation give their bouquet and their richness in natural sugar.

This agrarian civilization, which has constantly renewed itself through the centuries, has slowly created a Catalan type, half way between the wildness of the mountain dweller and the civility of the man of the plain, a man both tied to his traditions and open to outside influences,

Peach trees in flower in the Spring, plain of Roussillon.

24

hard working and gay. The Catalan language, which has for centuries provided the link between Roussillon and Spanish Catalonia, has suffered on this side of the Pyrenees from the influence of the French language. But the people still talk the language and the young are starting to find in it the new elements of an identity.

Although the Roussillon people have adapted well to their century, they still have that Mediterranean characteristic of living well and of games, which find their expression in rugby, in popular festivities or in family reunions accompanied by a good meal and wine.

Above: The Conflent and the mountain of Canigó (2731 meters) from the road between Sornià and Prada.
To the side: Artichoke flower.
To the right: The plain of Roussillon early in the morning, near Cornellà del Bèrcol.

Following pages: Market in Elna.

Perpignan

The capital of Roussillon and today of the département of the Pyrénées-Orientales does not have an old history but it is a very rich and varied one. Its golden century was without a doubt the thirteenth when Perpignan became the capital of the kingdom of Mallorca. The advantage of neighbouring ports and of the cloth trade enriched the town. The shipowners established their stock exchange in the Llotja de Mar, transformed today into a café. The town's francization after the Treaty of the Pyrenees has not taken away its Catalan personality. The recent growth of the town has not subtracted from the vitality of the historical centre. It is there that people from the whole of Roussillon come to do their shopping and there are situated the big cafés where everyone meets. It is also there that since the fifteenth century the great Easter procession has passed. A procession in which the men, dressed in black or red

Above: Perpignan, procession La Sang (blood) of Good Friday.
To the right: Beginning of the procession

in front of the cathedral of Sant Joan.
Following pages: Penitents of the Blood and Christ of the Cross (14th C.).

To the left: Perpignan, palace of the king of Mallorca, the hall of the throne (14th C.).

Gothic galleries of the elegant courtyard of honour of the palace.

hoods, carry images and the women, covered in black lace veils, represent all the scenes from the Passion. It is an occasion which is deeply marked by baroque realism and Spanish mysticism; similar events take place in lots of other Catalan towns.

Surviving in Perpignan from this period are the following buildings: the Castellet, Santa Maria de la Real, which was a royal church, Sant Jaume, cathedral of the order of the Blood (Blood of Christ) and above all the Palace of the kings of Mallorca. Built in the 13th and 14th centuries by James the Conqueror and his successor James II, its style is similar to that of the Generalitat of Barcelona, the abbadial palace of Vilabertran and the Royal Palace of Barcelona. This royal residence, which was disfigured and later abandoned, is a fine example of civil Catalan gothic architecture. A careful restoration which is still in process is restoring it slowly to its original state. The elegant interior courtyard, embellished with a double gallery, has become a magnificent site for Summer concerts.

The Red Coast

From Salanca to Argelers the coast is
a long succession of lagoons and beaches
which have been prepared for tourism
according to the plan
"Languedoc-Roussillon". Canet,
Barcarés, and Sant Cebrià have sprung up
from nothing from the sand. In Argelers
the landscape changes abruptly. The
Albera, covered by vineyards, pines and
holmoaks descends one thousand meters
from its peak to the sea. In the folds of the
Albera some villages like Cotlliure,
Portvendres, Banyuls and Cervera de la
Marenda, have found refuge since
antiquity. The famous profile of Cotlliure,
and of its Genovese tower dating from the
12th century, has become imprinted in the
popular imagination since Matisse,
Derain, Dufy, Marquet and others have
drawn this little port, which is no doubt
one of the most charming of the
Mediterranean coast.
Initially a Phoenician colony, later an
Iberian and Roman centre, Cotlliure,
"Cauco-Illiberis", has had in the course of
its history a great variety of master, until
Louis XIII, who conquered it in person,
made it for ever French.
The 17th century church, and its
altarpiece by Josep Sunyer, the Royal
Castle, a summer residence of the kings of
Mallorca, the fort of Sant Elm, erected by
Charles V, the old town whith its blue
façades, the limpid light of this coast,
combine to create the graphic poem of
Cotlliure which has been copied again and
again.
Tourism has made Cotlliure into
a fashionable port but they still fish for
sardines and anchovies. Fishing with
bright lights, which provides the
possibility of fishing during the night, has
been authorized again, and a curious
phenomenon is that one sees boats with
Latin-style sails again. A few kilometers
away, Portvendres, the old "Portus
Veneris" (port of Venus), lies, lamenting
its great period of prosperity when North
Africa was French. Yachts have replaced
the big cargo ships.
Banyuls, the town of Maillol, surrounded
by the vineyards responsible for its
famous wine, which cover all the sides,
even the most insignificant slopes, of the
Albera, and further away of Cervera,
which protects the frontier like the Cerber
of the Greek mythology, with its beaches,
warm waters and palm trees, announces
the Costa Brava.

*Cotlliure, the port and the beach seen from
the royal castle.*

Above: Cotlliure, petanque being played at the foot of the royal castle.
Castle of Cornellà del Bèrcol (12th C.).
Spraying vineyards.

To the right: a meal on the 14th of July in Bula d'Amunt.

The Romanesque Renaissance

After the bleak times of the great
invasions which swept away the Roman
Empire and desolated the north of
Catalonia, Roussillon sank into the great
darkness of a time traumatized by the idea
of the end of the world. The year 1000
liberated spirits and announced an artistic
awakening of a vast number of countries,
from north Italy to Catalonia. This sudden
outburst, the ramification of which spread
to the Alps and the Rhine valley,
provoked a real renaissance in the Catalan
countries from the 10th to the 13th
century.
The Roussillon, the valleys of the
Pyrenees and the north of Catalonia,
liberated from the Arabs and reintegrated
in the western world, are covered by
a white mantle of churches. It is the
triumph of Romanesque art. In the
Roussillon this art, although much
influenced by its Italian origins, has its
own style. Even though they have been
very abandoned there are still enough
romanesque monuments in the Roussillon
to follow the development of this style.
The end of the 19th century and the
beginning of ours did not respect this
inheritance at all. The chapels and
sanctuaries were all in ruins, the cloister of
Sant Genís de Fontanes was sold to the
Philadelphia Museum of Art and that of
Sant Miquel de Cuixà went to New York
where it became "The Cloisters" of the
Metropolitan Museum.
The reaction no doubt came from the
other side of the Pyreneès where from
1860 they began to assemble in Vic,
Barcelona and Girona the great

*Above, to the left: Majesty, detail of the
lintel (11th C.) of Sant Genís de Fontanes;
to the right: Christ in wood (14th C.),
church of Vilafranca de Conflent.
To the right: the plain of Elna; on the
horizon, the peak of Canigó.*

collections of the Catalan Museums. Between the fifties and seventies almost all the romanesque buildings of Roussillon have been restored.

The first buildings in the romanesque style were made by itinerant masons and stand out on account of their sobriety and total lack of ornamentation. The expansion of the cult of relics caused the aparition of crypts and subterranean churches, as at Sant Martí del Canigó.

Later everywhere, at Sant Miquel de Cuixà, at Cornellà de Conflent, at Elna, at Millars, at Sant Pere de Roda they built those square or rectangular towers, often pierced by windows which are the sign of adherence to this new art style. The lintel of Sant Genís de Fontanes, which it has been possible to attribute to the year 1020, represents the beginning of Roussillon sculpture.

The drawing of the Pantocrator is not deeply engraved in the marble and the style is still reminiscent of the Gallo-Roman tombs.

We find something similar but less gracious with the lintel of Sant Andreu de Sureda. In this way, slowly, genuine sculptors established themselves who worked near the marble quarries and furnished the chapels of the region with capitals, columns and engraved stones. Its masterpiece is Serrabona.

Situated in the barren and dry region of Aspres, this priory was consecrated around 1150 and nothing in its simple exterior betrays the existence of the treasure inside: the tribune. This piece, carved in pink marble, shows in the firmness of the drawing and the richness of the iconography illustrating the mythology of the medieval ages, the long way romanesque art had moved in a few years. This unique piece, in which technical perfection is attained, is in contrast with its sober surroundings, almost too small for it; it is for this reason that sometimes it has been thought that the tribune was not originally intended for Serrabona but for another church in Roussillon.

Everywhere around, from the coast to the high Cerdanya, the artists of those days, be they sculptors, painters or architects, left important works, sometimes marked with their names: Elna and its cloister, the tympanum of Cabestany (the work of the master of Cabestany), the frescoes of Sant Martí de Fenollar, the architecture and capitals of Sant Miquel de Cuixà, the lay-out of the Chapel of Planes, the policromated furniture of Angostina and

Abbey of Sant Martí del Canigó.

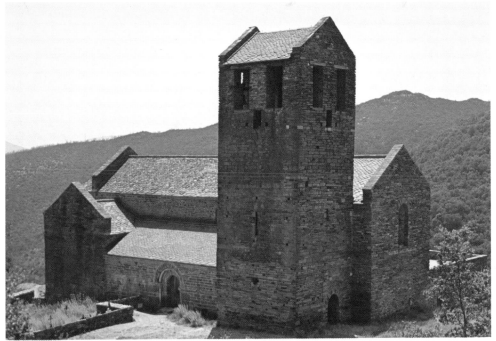

many others as well.

One is often surprised by the quality of the sites chosen by the religious orders for the buildings of their churches: it is necessary to have seen Sant Miquel de Cuixà and particularly Sant Martí del Canigó, both hidden in the mountain valleys, to understand better the atmosphere of monastic life in the Middle Ages.

That life, which for a long time had abandoned the monasteries, has been partly renewed today. Sant Miquel de Cuixà has had again since 1965 a religious order from Montserrat and its role as a spiritual and artistic centre has revived. Sant Martí del Canigó was saved fifty years ago by Monsegnor Carsalade du Pont, bishop of Elna and Perpignan. Its restored buildings, (restored a bit too systematically), its high and beautiful situation, and the surrounding chestnut woods, make it an ideal place for reunions or spiritual relaxation. The Angel Sant Miquel also likes high altitudes.

To the left: Priory of Serrabona, tribune of pink marble.
Above: Detail of a capital.

Bottom: Exterior of the priory.
Following pages: Chapel of La Coma; to the right, the peak of Canigó.

LLEIDA

It is not a long time ago that economically speaking the lands of Lleida were fairly insignificant. Today it is the larder of this country. A great step forward has been achieved. You must have noticed that arriving at Cervera, for example, you enter a sort of calm and atony. You can feel the calm, the atony of agrarian life. It is not disagreeable. On the contrary it is invigorating. Would it be accurate to say that this area is all the same and looks uniform? No. Some areas in this region show real movement and activity. The capital itself, Lleida, still presided over by the impressive volume of La Seu Vella (the cathedral) fully restored, is already a big city, and one of great quality and intense vitality. Other towns around show the same spirit. Stop in Tàrrega, Balaguer and other towns. You will see it. The great event for this area, maybe the greatest in its history, has been the construction of canals, the irrigation which is the characterizing feature of its agriculture. It took a long time for these to be completed but the will was there. The lands of the province of Lleida are today one of the greatest resources of this country. Everything is a question of continuing, conserving, increasing. The contrast between the calmness of the agrarian areas and the essential activity for their fertility is the essence of this area. The contrast between the state of these areas not long ago and their state now is

Coll de Nargó, romanesque chapel of Sant Climent.

admirable. Surprising? No doubt. Lleida has an economy which enjoys the best of prospects – on the up, increasingly prosperous, perhaps the most firmly based resource of our country.

Reservoir of Oliana on the river Segre.

Unfortunately I don't have the knowledge on Lleida which I have more or less about other areas of the country. I don't have a good overall view. Maybe I know the north better than the south, which I regret. Maybe I know Tremp better than Mollerussa.

In the north of this region they have made a considerable effort to exploit the rivers for hydroelectric power. This is something which is always fascinating. There are the two Pallars plants, the high and the low, the Jussa and the Sobira. I have friends who have helped me to understand the system. I have a great admiration for Sr. Boixareu, who today is the representative of the ministry of commerce in New York. He has taught me a lot of things. He is objective, speaks without rhetoric or false illusions, and how fond he is of his country! I remember visiting him with Joan Sardà, who has studied monetarism. The visit was marvellous, and above all for gastronomic reasons. Those trouts we used to eat in the country houses with local black mushrooms of the area, it was summer time, how delicious they were. I have forgotten the name of the village like so many things in my life. Forgetfulness is lack of spirit, imbecility. I also made a lot of good friends in that mountain village. I am not very keen on mountains, in fact, despite their being so high and impressive! A poet wrote: "There is nothing in this whole world like the mountains". Fair enough, I have always lamented the lack of plains in Catalonia. The country would be much richer with more of them. Still this is the reality and it is best that I don't write anything more about the prodigious region of Lleida.

J.P.

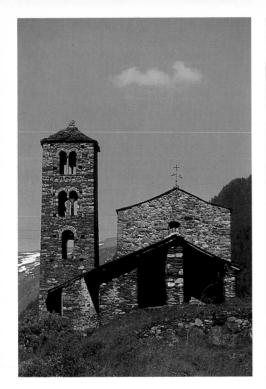

Andorra

"The Great Charlemagne, my father, liberated me from the Arabs... alone, I remain the only daughter of the Emperor Charlemagne." These first words of the Andorran national anthem summarize all the history of the last seigneurie of a feudal type in the west. The co-principality of Andorra was born of the agreement of "Pariatge" (sharing) drawn up in 1278 by the bishop of Urgell and Roger Bernat III, count of Foix, which established as co-princes the bishop of Urgell and the count of Foix.

This system of government has survived wars and revolutions during eleven centuries with only one change: inheritances have caused the French half of the co-sovereignty to be transferred to the kingdom of France, by Henry IV, and today to be exercised by the president of the Republic.

The country of the valleys of Andorra, isolated from France for a long time by a ring of peaks of around three thousand meters height, is more accessible from the

Above, to the left: Andorra, romanesque chapel of Sant Joan de Caselles; to the right: Market of Seu d'Urgell.
To the side: Seu d'Urgell, apse of the cathedral.
To the right: Andorra, sides of Pas de la Casa on the way up to Port d'Envalira.

south, via the river Segre. It is an integral part of the Catalan world. It is besides the only nation in which Catalan is the official language. With the opening of the road coming from France, the establishment of Summer tourism and Winter sports and the fact of being a tax free zone, the pastoral economy and the way of life of the valleys of Andorra have been completely transformed...

In a few years the populations has doubled, the shepherds have become shopkeepers, the pastures have been covered by hotels and ski-lifts, and Andorra Vella the capital, formerly a mountain village, is today with the "Escaldes", a long commercial street where you can buy everything free of tax. There survive from Andorra's eternal middle age beautiful romanesque buildings like Sant Joan de Caselles or Santa Coloma with its superb cylindrical tower, and the Andorrans, a bit submerged by the waves of the new residents, retain a pride in being different, free and rich.

Above, to the left: gate of a pyrenean cemetery; to the right: Gorge of la Noguera Pallaresa near Pobla de Segur.
To the right: Coll de Nargó, romanesque chapel of Sant Climent.

The Vall d'Aran

The Vall d'Aran is the highest valley formed by the Garonne which has its source in the glaciers of the Maladeta range of mountains and becomes Catalan by crossing a valley before flowing northwards to fertilize the plains of Occitania.

We had to wait until 1925, when the king Alfonso XIII had the road of the pass of Bonaigua made, for there to be communications between the Aran valley and the province of Lleida and Spanish nation. In the course of its history, separated from the influence of neighbouring nations, the Vall d'Aran formed its character and its own culture. They talk aranés there, which is close to Catalan but originates in Gascon. They are "aranesos" before being Catalan or Spanish.

Not longer than twenty years ago the aranesos lived of their sheep and a bit of tourism from France. Tourism, the wintersports and the hydroelectric energy have again determined the life of the valley. With the opening in 1948 of the tunnel of Viella, which makes the Vall d'Aran accessible in all seasons, as well as establishing communications between France and Spain, everything has changed. The urban necessity of fresh air propels a large number of the inhabitants

Les Bordes, in the Vall d'Aran, pyrenean houses with the classic slate rooves.

54

of Barcelona, Lleida and Toulouse to the
skiing stations of Vaqueira and Salardú.
These people receive a weekly relaxation
in their second homes.
Viella, the little capital, has trebled its
population and its charm has gradually
modified. There is something which is
always fascinating about this area. This is
the water. Its universal presence in
waterfalls and little rivers, falling on the
rocks amongst the fir trees, crossing the
fields, makes it a paradise of purity and
high altitudes. From the other side of the
pass of de Bonaigua, or coming from the
valley of the Noguera Pallaresa, you come
through Espot to the national park of
Aigüestortes, which is overlooked by the
impressive peaks of the Encantats, which
are reflected in the waters of the lake of
Sant Maurici. It is one of the most
beautiful places of the Catalan Pyrenees
with a great variety of landscape,
vegetation and lakes. At 2900 meters of
altitude it is also the kingdom of deers,
wild goats and wildboars and perfect for
climbing. If you traverse the tunnel of
Viella, coming from the Vall d'Aran, you
will suddenly find yourself in a world of
minerals with no villages for miles, at the
feet of the Pyrenean giants of the
Maladeta: the high valley of the Noguera
Ribagorçana.

*Above: Els Encantats, national park of
Aigüestortes.*
*To the left: Upper valley of Noguera
Ribagorçana; beyond, the first heights of
mount Maladeta.*

The Valley of Boí

These high valleys were always alive with a movement to and fro of people from the most distant countries of Christendom. The artist and sculptors from the north of Italy, paid their way by working for a while on the decorations of a church. All the churches of the Pyrenees were born of this movement. In the valley of Boí a particular style developed in the 12th century, Pyrenean Romanesque with square naves rooved with wood and pointed towers, the different stories of the tower having double or triple arches and Lombard bands. The church of Erill-la-vall and above all Sant Climent and Santa Maria de Taüll represent the masterpieces of this style. Sant Climent and Santa Maria were both consecrated by Saint Ramon, bishop of Roda, in 1123 and they owe their fame to the elegance of their architecture and the beauty of their mural paintings the originals of which were taken to the Catalan Museum of Art in Barcelona.
The copies left in the churches, which are quite good ones, manifest all the refinement of style and the mastery of colour of the anonymous artists of the 12th century. These frescoes form an important part of Europe's great artistic heritage.

Above: Sant Climent de Taüll, Christ Pantocrator, copy of the fresco of the 12th century (the original is in the Museum of Art of Catalonia, in Barcelona).
To the left: Church of Sant Climent de Taüll with its tower of six storeys.

The Plateaux of Lleida

Below the high Pyrenean valleys the province of Lleida descends southwards in a succession of plateaux and plains which are deeply pierced by the beds of three rivers which have forced their way little by little through the rocky wall of Montsec. The Montsec is the mountain range which runs from west to east and which separates Pallars and Ribagorça from the low lands of Lleida. It is the geographical, and today economic, key of the lands of Lleida.

The waters of the Noguera Ribagorçana, those of the Noguera Pallaresa and, towards Urgell, those of the Segre have cut deep falls and gorges into the softer rocks where they have established hydroelectric works of great importance for Catalan industry and for the agriculture of the region.

The terrain was ideal for construction of reservoirs and for the retention of water. This presence of water has changed the landscape of these areas forming giant artificial lakes in the middle of the arid mountains, of an ocre or grey colouring which varies depending on the inclination of the sun. The water has transformed the agricultural economy totally. In the last century this region of continental climate, dry and warm in summer and cold and dry in winter, had only a subsistance agriculture based on a few ruined and poor villages. A wide range of irrigation systems distributes the waters of the three rivers and has made possible the development of a modern agriculture which exports its cereals, fruit and vegetables to the rest of the country and abroad.

The higher lands of the plateaux retain still their arid aspect, and this serves to reveal Aragon, but the presence of the olive tree, the vine and the first pines remind us that the Mediterranean is not far away.

The more fertile zones are further up than Lleida around Balaguer where the waters of the Pyrenean rivers mix together in the bed of the river Segre.

This fertile horticultural and fruit-growing plain and its little industries which have developed have given rise to expansion in Lleida, the capital, which previously was a bit sleepy and provincial in the shadow of its badly looked after cathedral.

Valley of the Noguera Ribagorçana, view of the mountain range of Sant Gervàs.

Lleida

Born on the top of a hill dominating the plain of the Segre, Lleida is of historical and geographical significance. Capital of the plain, it is the Western limit, the sentinel of the Principality, facing the arid lands of Aragon and the meeting point of the waters of the Pyrenees, the Mediterranean world and continental Spain. This position has caused Lleida, from Roman times until our days, to experience all the influences and a lot of destructions. The stones of the old fortification (the Suda) below the cathedral still show the wounds of these depredations, the last of which was in 1936.

Built from 1203 to 1278, on the site of an Arab mosque, the old Seu (cathedral), which has had all the styles plastered on it, has suffered from the depreciation shown since the 18th century for the romanesque and gothic styles.

The gothic cloister of the 14th century surprises by its position in front of the façade of the church. It reminds us of the

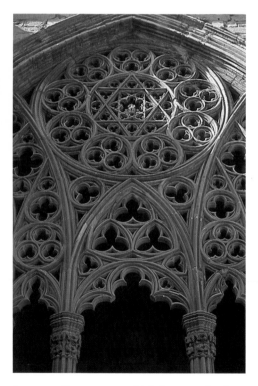

lay-out of mosques, which have patios in front of them. The exterior carvings on the church give us a good example of attractive combinations of different artistic styles: late romanesque art (gate of Fillols), Arab influence (gate of the Anunciata), gothic door frame of French style (gate of the Apostles).

The old town grouped around the Suda, has kept the Paeria, a beautiful romanesque building which has the Town Hall inside, and the Santa Maria hospital, of gothic style and today a museum.

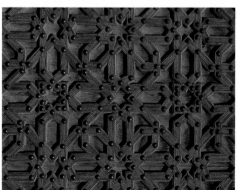

Above, to the left: Cathedral of Lleida, detail of the Gothic ornaments in the cloister; to the right: Window of the cloister above the town.
To the side: Adornment of the door of Fillols.
To the right: Lleida cathedral.

Following pages: Lleida, plaça de l'Ereta on a Sunday morning in Spring.

Girona

They say that the Girona region is the most beautiful in our country. It is a Summer idea which has been very widespread and very positive. Girona has everything: the most beautiful mountains, a beautiful plain and the famous Costa Brava, more or less damaged by tourism, which from Blanes to Portbou includes one hundred kilometers of little villages, beaches and unforgettable views. The Empordà, the big and the little one, is very famous and generally liked. Still if I could give away a present I would give away the climate of this country. I would give away all the tramontana winds of the Canigó, the mistral winds, the ones coming from Roses and those of the Golf du Lion or winds of Provence. I would also give away the Garbí winds which are sometimes unending, humid and produce useless and functionless sadnesses.

The city of Girona has a great personality, particularly because of its great religious buildings. The cathedral, built on a romanesque foundation, with a prodigious cloister, was qualified as "ersatz" by a great surgeon friend of mine that I took there. That is exact because it is the most important feudal ecclesiastical phenomenon in this country. The strength of Girona is the essence of this feudalism. In the cathedral there is a remarkable museum. The roof of the cathedral is very thin and is a remarkable architectural feature. Then there is the palace of the bishop, abandoned by the present bishop, Sant Feliu, the romanesque document of Sant Pere de Galligants, with a cloister that has been a provincial museum for many years, and the fortress of Montjuic, to the north of Girona. At the time of the Napoleonic invasion there were in Girona a lot of convents and rich houses of gentry who had left their villages and gone to live in Girona because of the lack of security in the villages. Nearly all the convents have been destroyed. In those days Girona must have looked terrifying and of a unique personality. Those were the elements which made the war with the French, and the general Álvarez de Castro who against military opinion resisted the attack of the enemy. In general the old streets have an agreeable, archaic look. The modern streets are simply to get to places. The French elements in Girona are the Devesa and the field of Març, for military instruction, Marshal de Saint-Cyr was

Figueres, sculpture by Salvador Dalí in front of the parish church of Sant Pere.

responsible for this. All the geography of Girona is military: the rivers crossing it, the stone walls and the plain to the west.

Girona is growing. You can see its industrialization. Its area has expanded and has been well administered. It has the second airport of Catalonia. The starting of the University is a positive thing and the fairs and markets are important. Around this area there are highly industrialized towns: Olot, Banyoles, Ripoll. Figueres is a nice frontier town. The Costa Brava is a unique world. Roses is the first in sea tourism, but who could forget Blanes, Lloret, Tossa, Sant Feliu de Guíxols? The villages of the cork industry were more important years ago but they haven't declined as much as they say. The industry of terracotta in the Bisbal is considerable. In this region there are two prodigious counties: the Empordà and the Selva. I do not mean the high Selva, a desert-like area on account of the bad fortune of the monastery de Sant Pere de Roda, but the Selva to the south of Girona. Perhaps these two counties are not as well cultivated as the Roussillon, but the beauty of its landscape is marvellous. I would recommend two months to see it: in May when everything is getting green and September when everything is turning golden. The Garrotxa is a magnificent region, more mountainous and lonely. Oh the little villages of my country! Pals has no rival. If one day you go to Cerdanya remember what the sculptor Manolo used to say: "The Cerdanya is the temple of nature". Its capital is Puigcerdà. The Guilleries are more rustic, but I would spend a lot of time there sitting near the fireside, reading or sleeping. In my country everyone always has something funny to say, which is essential in life.

J.P.

Santa Pau, Gothic window with coat of arms.
La Pera (Empordà), door of a masia (farm-house).

From the high valley of the river Ter to Girona

The counties of Girona are the most varied in Catalonia: the region has its head in the snows of the Pyrenees, its body lies in the plain of the Empordà, one foot lies in the warm waters of the Costa Brava and the other in the pine and oakwoods of La Selva.

Its Pyrenean head from Cerdanya to Cap de Creus is a range of high, peaks which has no opening until the pass of Le Perthus. The revival of the high valleys on both sides of the Pyrenees, emptied since the 19th century with the exodus towards the city, is a recent phenomenon. It dates from the birth of tourism and of winter sports. Since the roads have caused the skiing stations to be only a few hours away from the big cities of Catalonia, these villages, here as in Andorra or in the Vall d'Aran, have come to life again. A life which is certainly not so picturesque as the traditional image of mountain life but this is of course the price of progress.

Font-Romeu in the French Cerdanya and La Molina, Nuria and Vallter are expanding skiing resorts. They have the privilege of being the sunniest valleys of the Pyrenees. Not all the valleys have been lucky enough to have skiing pistes, or an important road, and in that case they remain as last refuges of an agrarian life nearing its end.

Above: Skiing in Vallter.
To the right: The upper valley of the river Ter, above Setcases.

The Catalans consider this part of the Pyrenees as a sacred land. It is here, Ripoll, that is the original home of the Catalan people. The Benedictine monastery of Santa Maria de Ripoll was founded in 888 by the first king-count of Catalonia, Wilfred the Hairy. Restored and enlarged afterwards, the abbot Oliba, bishop of Vic and Cuixà, caused it to progress considerably during the 11th century and enriched its architecture. During nine centuries Ripoll accumulated the richness, the works of art, the science and the memory of the Catalan people. The library and its archives were amongst the most important in Europe. The monastery and its abbots excercised their spiritual and intellectual influence over Catalonia but also on the whole of the West. This treasure of Catalonia's history was almost totally pillaged and burnt. The restoration in 1893 could only save the doorway and the cloister, considered the masterpieces of romanesque art of the eleventh century. The capitals of the cloister, and particularly the sculptures of the doorway, are a sort of illustrated story of the Medieval Ages. People could read all the passages in the Bible and the

Above to the left: Romanesque gate of Santa Maria de Ripoll; below: Romanesque lock of the church of Llanars and window surrounded by lions belonging to the church of Besalú.
Above: Besalú, romanesque fortified bridge.
To the side: Detail of a capital of the cloister of Ripoll.

Following pages: The mediaeval town of Santa Pau, near Olot.

History of the Church from its origins to its triumph as if they were an illustrated catechism. The county of Ripoll, and the east of the Garrotxa, protected by the complicated geography of the mountains, have conserved other testimonies of the Old Catalonia. There are anonymous memorials like the surprising village of Santa Pau, near Olot, where we find ourselves in a medieval ambiance. There are other better known places like the monastery of Sant Joan de les Abadesses, the bridge of Camprodon, the impregnable site of Castellfollit de la Roca and most definitely, the medieval Besalú.

Besalú was from the 9th to the 12th century capital of an independent county which stretched from Figueres to the Ter valley. Like all the towns in Catalonia, Besalú was commercially very alive during the entire Medieval Ages. In the 15th century the Jews dominated the economy of the county.

The religious toleration shown by the Catalans aided their integration and they made Besalú into the "Catalan Jerusalem", an active religious centre. You can get an idea of what Besalú was like in this period by walking across the fortified Roman bridge, today restored, which takes you through the narrow streets of the Jewish quarter to the centre where you can still see the tenth century synagogue and the beautiful Romanesque church. In Santa Pau, in Besalú, and in other villages some private associations have undertaken the difficult task of accurately restoring buildings.

The Catalan House

Near Olot and Vic the centuries have created a Catalan architectural style which we find with variations in other regions of Catalonia. It is everywhere dominated by the science of the vault inherited from the great periods of the Romanesque and Gothic architecture. Here in Ventós, a noble house close to Olot, marvellously preserved with its furniture by successive generations of the same family, we find in the foundations from the fifteenth century, and the staircase and double gallery of the 18th century, the whole range of this art.

Girona, city of the thousand sieges

The old "Gerunda", city of the thousand
sieges, built on a hill at the edge of the
meeting-point of the rivers Onyar and the
Ter, was always coveted by conquerors
because of its strategic situation.
It has Iberian, Roman, Visigothic, Arab
and medieval fortifications. La Chanson
de Roland records the attacks of
Charlemagne on the Arabs. The heroic
siege which Girona withstood for nine
months in front of Napoleonic troops is an
important historical fact.
Capital of its province with fifty thousand
inhabitants during the 19th century
Girona had to break its limits and cross
the river. In spite of this the old city, which
climbs the rocky hill in disorganized steps,
has kept all its medieval character.
A network of windy and narrow streets,
cut up by steps and surrounded at the sides
by irongates and doorways of noble
houses, lead to the cathedral. Contrary to
what one might think seeing its baroque

*Above: Girona, baroque façade and
doorway (17th C.) of the cathedral.
To the right: Old houses on the banks of
the river Onyar.*

façade at the top of a monumental
staircase, Girona cathedral is with its
sisters of Barcelona (the cathedral and
Santa Maria del Mar) the most important
monument of Catalonia. As in Barcelona
here too stands solemnly a church started
with three naves and finished with a sole,
central nave, which expresses the
individual genius of the Catalan
architects.

The tower of Charlemagne, the beautiful
romanesque cloister, and the Capitular
Museum, which has a rich collection of
first class religious works of art, both
romanesque and gothic, compose the area
around the cathedral. But the passing of
the centuries has not left Girona only the
Cathedral. Sant Feliu, Sant Pere de
Galligants, Sant Nicolau, Sant Domènec,
the Arab Baths and the old palaces form
an impressive monumental inheritance
which combines well, without
discordance, with the old centre.

At the side of the hill, the old houses next
to the Onyar and the Rambla with its
arcadas retain in Girona a particular

*Above: Girona, polychromated statue of
Saint Thomas of Aquinas (17th C.).
Capitular museum of the cathedral; the
Arab baths (12th C.).
To the right: Girona, the archaeological
promenade and the north area of the
cathedral.*

charm. Girona is a refined city, one of the highest achievement of our spirit.
City of monks and soldiers, artists and craftsmen and also industrial city made ugly in its modern part by incoherent and ungracious buildings, Girona has kept its character as the capital of Old Catalonia. The traditional Good Friday procession attracts a lot of people and they still dance sardanas near the Ramblas in the evenings.

Above: A house of the old town painted in relief.
Below: A "Cobla" (Sardana orchestra).

To the right: Bridge and houses on the river Onyar in the evening; Behind: the tower of the cathedral.

L'Empordà

In Catalonia, mainly a mountainous country, plains are rare. The one of the Empordà to the south of the Albera is by its geography, first cousin to the one of the Roussillon. A plain created by alluvial deposits from the Pyrenees. The Ter which irrigates and fertilizes it is its "Tree of life". A long time before the Via Augusta, the great Roman road which linked Rome with Tarragona and connected this area with the civilized world, the Empordà was only accessible by sea. It was by sea that the Greeks of Marseilles came to Empúries. It is also via the sea that the Romans began the romanization of the Peninsula. Lots of different peoples came, one after the other from the north and from the south. Some only passed through like the Arabs, others seduced by this hospitable and rich land stayed for ever. Here as well, in the year one thousand, the year of the Christian reconquest and feudalism, there was a renaissance.

The Empordà, church and tower of Sant Feliu de Boada.

83

Villages were formed around the churches and castles and the work on the land increased. This beginning established the major characteristics of the Empordà of today. The impression made by the Romans and Christians was strong enough for this country to retain its unity and personality. For the Empordà is not at all like the rest of the counties of the Principality. The living standards are significantly higher, the inhabitants are open-hearted, the climate is different because of the influences of the sea and the landscape formed of large corn fields and tinted with lines of cypresses, olive trees, pines, evergreen oaks and vineyards is indeed very latin.

The miracle of the Empordà lies in the fact that up to now it has been able to escape the disasters of tourism. There are some villages like La Bisbal, Figueres and Palafrugell which have grown in the last twenty years but the villages have not changed much. The coast has changed much more.

The millions of tourists who come to this coast every year are looking for the sun, the sea and the sand, but how many of them realize that a few miles away there is a world of a softer grace where things don't move so fast? This ignorance has contributed no doubt to prolonging here a style of life, traditions and beliefs and

The Empordà, church of Peratallada.

the same physical appearance. Away from the great movements of the century the most beautiful medieval villages like Pals, Peratallada, Monells or Cruïlles have awoken today from their gracious ruins thanks to the passion their old stones have aroused. Barcelona and Girona people and foreigners who love this country, artists and craftsmen, have brought life back to these stoned streets, to the old castles, and to the beautiful peasant farms, so many centuries old.

The archaeological treasure of the Empordà is rich with a lot of villages almost always built on hills dominating the land around. The profile of their ochre roofs, of their walls, towers or belfries; the dark green stains of the cypress trees contrasting with the stone, and the transparent light, are the ingredients of a fragile harmony which gives the impression of eternal peace.

Apart from its old stones the Empordà has kept its old customs, festivities and skills for crafts. A traditional type of agrarian

Above, to the left: Olive tree; to the right aeriel view of the High Empordà.
At the side: A street of Flaçà.
To the right: Aerial view of the mediaeval town of Peratallada.

economy has conserved all sorts of trades which have disappeared in the more modernized regions like: smiths, ironworkers and wheelwrights.

The local masons still know how to make vaulted roofs in the Catalan way. We find as well stone-masons and sculptors and the art of ceramic, in all its forms, is very alive again because of the recent demand created by tourism. In all Catalonia even the smallest village celebrates every year the fête of its patron saint but some of them still celebrate religious festivities dating from the Middle Ages. In Verges, for four hundred years, the Thursday night before Good Friday, the inhabitants relive Christ's Passion. On a little stage, placed in the middle of the little village square, the men, women and children of the village transformed, for one night, into JesusChrist, Maria Magdalen, Pontius Pilate or even a Roman centurion, play their roles. That night the narrow streets are lit with torches except for one of the streets in which they light, when the procession arrives, all the oil lamps fixed to the walls. Christ, carrying his cross, is preceded by a curious, macabre dance in which Death armed with scythe and the skeletons which serve him jump up and down to the rhythm of drums.

Verges: Easter Thursday procession, the macabre dance.

88

This demonstration, in which the sacred and the profane mix, is unique because of its strictly popular participation. Because of its originality thousands of people go to see it. The peasants still inhabit magnificent fortified houses in the Empordà, often adjoining a tower, a reminder of Moorish attacks, and with wonderfully sculptured gothic windows and beautiful doors framed with heavy iron fringes. Some old peasants still work the vineyards with mules. But altogether these are just the last remains of a dying world. Here as well agriculture has been modernized in the last few years... yields make this necessary. It is important to say that in this region, like in the Roussillon, everything grows: wheat, corn, fruit trees, vegetables and even rice, although that has been now abandoned because of scarcity of labour. It is a land of arable but also of livestock, with lots of sheep which pasture on the moorland or on the plain recovered from the sea, near Roses, Empúries and Torroella de Montgrí.

You cannot leave the Empordà without visiting Figueres capital of the High Empordà, the Dalí Museum, the brilliant surrealist "happening" of this celebrated son of the region. Nor must you forget some of the splendid inheritances of the Catalan Golden Age: the monastery of Vilabertran, the cathedral of Castelló d'Empúries, the castle of Perelada and particularly the monastery of Sant Pere de Roda.

Plain of the High Empordà, sheep-raising near Castelló d'Empúries.

A five thousand year old art

Some of the sources are old Egyptian, Persian and Chinese and these formed the origin of a ceramic art which afterwards obtained a European monopoly in the 14th and 15th centuries, and survived until the explosion of the modern style. During the industrial revolution Catalan ceramics diversified considerably. The artisanal work continued in traditional centres like La Bisbal. The wood-fired oven disappeared and the turning wheel came to function with a motor but the quality of the clay, the way of working it, and baking it have not changed.

Above: Ceramics, working with the turning wheel, painting and exhibition of wares made by artisans of la Bisbal.
Below: Lead bath which creates the varnish after the baking process.

Sant Pere de Roda

It is one of the last villages of the Pyrenees, whence you can view all the coast from Cervera to Cap de Creus. It is a moorland of difficult access.

This sober and sumptious site and the legends around it have always excited the imagination. The history of Sant Pere de Roda started probably during the last years of the Visigothic Empire when Boniface IV was Pope. Frightened of an invasion from the East, the Pope decided to send the valuable relics of the apostles Peter and Paul and other martyrs to more secure places. It is believed that the remains were hidden in a cave situated underneath the major altar of the church and that later they were sent back to Rome. The first Benedictan monastery dates from the 10th century; it was destroyed and rebuilt various times and definitely abandoned in the 18th century. Saved from ruin by a light restoration, the collection of buildings now forms a monument of pure romanesque tradition, very like those of the Roussillon, like Elna, Vilafranca de Conflent or Cuixà.

Above: Monastery of Sant Pere de Roda, romanesque tower of the church.
To the left: From the site of the monastery you get a view of Port de la Selva and the beginning of the Costa Brava.

The Costa Brava

Between the French border and Blanes, looking to the sea, and along the entire length of the Girona region for a hundred kilometers, there is a rock formation of rose colour and abrupt form which has earned the name of the "Costa Brava". The name was invented about fifty years ago.

There is not one Costa Brava but two. The one of yesterday and that of today. They relate to each other like two hostile sisters and we know that the younger one will devour the older one. When, at the beginning of the century, some artists, seduced by the beauty of Cadaqués, made their summer retreat in that fishing village, they didn't realize that they were blazing the path for a sunthirsty European invasion. Tossa was another such place. The first tourists discovered something which seemed to them like a lost paradise: some white villages, slumbering in the shelter of bays, agreeable fishing and rural villages, a warm and transparent sea,

welcoming beaches and the almost biblical peace of this Mediterranean coast, forgotten by progress.

Very quickly tourist publicity sent the images and names of Cadaqués, Roses, Empúries, L'Estartit, Platja d'Aro, Tossa de Mar or Calella to the four corners of Europe. Of the old Costa Brava Cadaqués is the best preserved symbol.

It is true anyway that with the presence of Salvador Dalí, Henry François Rey, Josep Pla and all the artists, writers, cinema people from Marcel Duchamp to Buñuel who have walked along its white streets

Above and to the side: Cadaqués, narrow street of the old quarter, the church and the beach.
To the right: Cadaqués, aeriel view of Podritxó, the Poal and the Pianc.

Following pages: Riba Pitxot, Port Alguer and the Baluard.

and its polyglot cafés, Cadaqués awoke soom to its graces. This Catalan Saint-Tropez, permanently fashionable, where the "intelligentsia" and the distinguished drop-outs of the Costa Brava meet. The avant-garde, paradoxically, have protected tradition.

It is here in Empúries, between Roses and l'Escala, that everything started. Founded in the 5th century before Christ by the Greeks who came from Marseilles a first "Emporium", factory and store-house, was established at what is today Sant Martí d'Empúries. To expand the colony settled on the coast and created the new town (Neapolis) of which modern excavations have revealed the principal public places. Empúries became Roman when Cornelius and Scipio landed to cut-off the rearguard of the Carthaginian, Hannibal. The Roman conquerors settled down in Empúries and they extended the town, creating a new town further up from the Greek one.
Romanization extended to all Catalonia and to the rest of the Iberic Peninsula. There are some very old and beautiful remains of the times of the Caesars:

a house with its mosaic, the "atri" and "peristil" (ancestor of the patio), the ruins of a forum, remains of an amphitheatre and some beautiful archaeological pieces on show either in the Museum of

Above: Empúries, Roman house.
Below: The Roman Forum.
To the right: aerial view of the Greek city, (Neapolis).

Empúries or in that of Barcelona. In this typical Mediterranean spot, with its sea pines and cypress trees, you suddenly obtain a real vision of the Ancient world. Even more than the stones it is that which is the seduction of Empúries.

In the same way as Empúries, all the coast, until the third century B. C., lived within the Roman peace. Then there came the great invasions from the north (the first ones) which broke up a five century old civilization. In 802 Charlemagne repelled the Arabs and integrated the region to the Spanish March. The medieval period, with the triumph of the Church, saw the birth of a lot of ports: Sant Feliu de Guíxols, Torroella de Montgrí, Palamós. To protect themselves from the Moors and other pirates who would often devestate the coast, they built everywhere forts, watchtowers, fortified houses and walls.
These defence signs still mark the landscape of the Costa Brava and its back country. The touristic invasion of the 20th century is very different from the invasions before the Middle Ages. Its sin is more a result of a constructing madness

Above: S'Agaró, the Hostal de la Gavina and its gardens.
To the side: L'Estartit, preparations for the 1979 world championship of "Minitons".
To the right: Cala Pedrosa, between l'Escala and l'Estartit.

rather than of a destructive one.
There is nothing one can do about the disfigured places but the time has perhaps come to be aware of what has happened. There has been a fight, likewise without success, to save Aigua-Xellida one of the last virgin bays of Palafrugell from tourist promotion. In some areas you cannot build any more and they have established some urban plans for all these villages which have become authentic Summer cities. But today there is a general belief amongst people that it has been carried too far. But the Costa Brava of today cannot escape its vocation of holiday zone. It is irreversible. Each village equips itself and specializes. Roses has grown considerably and apart from its fishing port has an important pleasure port.

Following pages: Sportive port of l'Estartit.

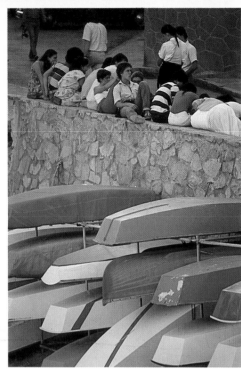

L'Escala extends itself the other side of the hill. L'Estartit, with its strange emplacement between the rocks of Roca Maura and Medes islands, enlarges its sailing port every year. Pals has a superb golf centre which attracts people from all around. The bays of Begur and Palafrugell, hidden amongst rocks, have not changed much. S'Agaró has invested a lot in its luxury hotel and its palatial villas, and has thus saved its landscape; Platja d'Aro is a night-club in the pine woods; Palamós, Sant Feliu and Lloret line up their hotels behind the old villages and it's a long time ago that Tossa grew beyond its walls.

The permanent resource of this area is its climate. The weather is always good and freshened by the sea winds, the gregal or the garbi, or purified by the tramontana. It is the place for sea sports.

Water-skiing, sailing, regattas, under water fishing etc. It is also the ideal place for family holidays. You can always choose between the beach and the neighbouring bays where you can isolate yourself as long as you have something which floats. You can also choose, depending on financial resources, between luxury villa or camping site.

Above: A wall for watching the sea.
To the right: General view of Calella de Palafrugell and of the Port Bo.

106

Apart from the old people of the area, whom we find sometimes grouped together near the port, looking a bit shocked by a cataclysm which they have not understood, every one else has profited from the touristic boom. The local people have become richer from the millions of tourists who spend here the holidays of their dreams and pay a good price, and the whole of Spain has gained from this "manna" of foreign currency which has provided the means for balancing the nation's terms of trade. The old wooden boats lined up on the beach, the nice colourful sails on the blue sea, the half rural, half maritime rhythm, the songs of the fishermen in the cellars, the sardanas in the square or in the main street, form part now of the museum (still to be formed) of the Costa Brava. Let us hope that those nostalgic of the old times console themselves thinking that tourism has opened the area to a multitude of liberal influences which no doubt have contributed to the strengthening of its identity.

Above and at the side: Returning from fishing at Palamós.
Following pages: Aeriel view of Tossa de Mar; to the right, the old town.

Barcelona

Today Barcelona, on account of its population and its touching the sea, is the most important city of the Mediterranean. Marseilles is full but smaller. Genoa has some strength. Then there must come Athens, growing considerably and finally perhaps there is Naples. I am talking of towns on the sea. Neither Rome nor Cairo are on the sea.

Personally I prefer old Barcelona to the new but this is not important. When they opened the big street Layetana and destroyed a good part of the old Barcelona if I had known anything at the moment I am sure that I would have been against it. It was done by the modernists, who always want changes, and who perhaps have the instinct of destruction, which has been practised so much in this country. I like curved streets, which are the most elegant and provide constant surprises. The projection of the Cerdà plan for the enlarging of Barcelona produced very long streets, unending, and of a terrible monotony. There is not a single house the same, not even in height, because everything has to be different and personal. The old quarter of Barcelona, called the Gothic quarter, is admirable.

Barcelona is an important city commercially and industrially and has considerable life and movement. But apart from the city itself all the surrounding areas are industrialized. Particularly the last section of the river Llobregat and the towns behind: Martorell, Terrassa, Sabadell, Ripollet, Granollers, which form a big concentration of a phenomenal volume. And what about the Maresma along the coast? It never ends. Together with big and little factories they have built huge blocks of flats. They have changed a great part of the landscape of the country. Have they not gone a bit too far?

Barcelona, beyond the zone just mentioned which extends to the south, north and west, has another zone further out: Vilanova, Igualada, Manresa, Berga and further still Vic. More and more people move to Barcelona every day. To go to Barcelona is a sort of ideal. It seems they like it. I wish them a good stay.

Barcelona, modernist ticket office of the Palau de la Música Catalana.

Barcelona, the avenue of Columbus in 1900.
Below: Miró Foundation: sculpture by Miró.

The only quick and clear exit out of Barcelona is the Penedès. The landscape of this country is very fractured but there are vineyards, which solve everything when they are green and when in the autumn they turn red after the vendange. Vilafranca del Penedès is an unforgettable town and in a very good condition.

One must remember that in Catalonia, presiding over the country, there are two great geological faults: the mountain of the Montseny and that of Montserrat. The Montseny is destined to be the natural park of Barcelona. We find it a few miles away from the big city, isolated and beautiful countryside which was celebrated in the songs of the poet Gerau de Liost in his book *La muntanya d'ametistes*. On Montserrat, a unique mountain because of the originality and picturesqueness of its shape, is situated our Benedictan monastery and our patron Virgin. A visit there is mandatory.

Maybe I have not lived enough in Barcelona to have found out all its charms. In all I have lived there, as a young student and as a miserable journalist, five or six years. Barcelona has great appeal. I like old Barcelona, the cathedral, the marvellous church of Santa Maria del Mar, the gothic quarter, the Rambla, the square of the Pine, the Opera house and its club (the Liceu), the traditional things.

I like the Rambla de Catalunya because it has plane trees. The Passeig de Gràcia is perhaps a bit too broad but I may be wrong. The Diagonal is too much for me. You can still find some quality shops, not many. Anyway we would never finish. The climate of the lower part of Barcelona is not so good as that of the higher part where the air is cleaner.

J.P.

LA PIEDAD DEL SEÑOR
JAIME GUARDIA
HACIA 1500

Vic

In the centre of a big plain surrounded by mountains which isolate it from maritime influences, Vic — then known as Ansa — was in ancient times the capital of a great Iberian tribe. Today it is an important commercial and industrial centre (mainly textile) famous for its pork products and for its treasures from medieval Catalonia. Even though its history has been violent (Vic has been frequently damaged) it preserves some valuable relics of its long existence: a Roman temple of the 2nd century, almost perfect, discovered by chance in 1882, during the demolition of the old palace of the Montcada family; the romanesque crypt of 1038 discovered too by chance during the restoration of the

Above: Episcopal Museum at Vic, Piety by Jaume Guàrdia (around 1500).
To the left: The bringing down from the Cross (12th C.) of Erill-la-vall, one of the master-pieces in this museum.

115

ET·PERTRANSII

cathedral which was burnt during the civil war; a great arcaded square, where all the old streets of the old town meet, some fine examples of civil architecture from the 14th and 15th centuries, and particularly the area of the cathedral with its romanesque tower, gothic cloister and reconstructed neoclassic nave from the beginning of the 19th century.

Vic, however, retains two major surprises for the visitor: the Episcopal Museum, founded in 1891 by the bishop Morgades, which possesses some essential examples of Catalan Romanesque and Gothic art and the monumental frescoes of the cathedral to which the painter Josep Maria Sert devoted a large part of his life from 1930.

Around Vic, chapels like Sant Pere de Casserres, Sant Martí del Brull or Santa Maria de l'Estany, erected after the 10th century by the triumphant church, demonstrate even today the vitality of the romanesque art of this area which as in Taüll or Frontanyà, spread to the most solitary sites in a large number of monasteries, churches and cloisters.

To the left: Vic, nave of the cathedral and the frescoes by Josep Maria Sert.
Above: detail of a fresco.
Below, to the left: detail of the alabaster altar-piece by Pere Oller 1420; to the right: Episcopal Museum, Virgin with child, 12th century.

Montserrat

In all civilizations the popular interest in mysticism expresses itself by by looking for the sublime in exceptional places. Montserrat has been the sacred mountain of the Catalans for nine centuries. Certainly this huge block of granite sculptured by the water and the winds, in brutal and fantastic forms, lends itself naturally to spirituality. This mountain, which inspired Wagner in his decoration of *Parsifal*, has been inhabited since the

first preachings of the evangelists.
People searching the path to sanctity,
those who flee from persecution, have
multiplied the number of little hermitages
in inaccessible parts of the mountain or on
its vertical cliffs.

In the 9th century, one of the five little
hermitages, the tiny church of Santa
Maria, was offered to the Benedictines of
Ripoll and in 1025 the abbot Oliba,
a descendant of Wilfred the Hairy, Abbot
of Ripoll and of Sant Martí del Canigó,
bishop of Elna and of Vic, one of the

*Above: Montserrat, gallery of the grand
esplanade of the monastery opening onto
the mountain.
To the left, above: The monastery and the
gothic cloister, below: The exterior square.*

strongest personalities of romanesque Catalonia, founded the monastery of the Mother of God of Montserrat, dedicated to the Virgin. He built the original church and organized the monastic life.

The new sanctuary soon grew bigger and the Romanesque building had to be amplified in the 13th century. After becoming independent of Ripoll in 1409 the abbey attracted more pilgrims because of the erudition of its monks and its wealth. Famous people are included amongst the abbots and guests of Montserrat. James I went there to pray before the conquest of Majorca; Charles V made more than nine visits, Giuliano della Rovere, the future pope Julius II, patron of the masters of Italian renaissance, was one of its Abbots. Each century added a new building, a new treasure, until the troops of Napoleon pillaged everything in 1811 leaving hardly anything of the old abbey.

There remainst the mountain, the monastic spirit and above all the sacred image of the Moreneta (the Brownie), the black virgin of Montserrat, a polychromated statue of the 12th century which legend has it, was found in a cave of Montserrat by two shepherds,

and which has inspired universal devotion from medieval times. The present monastery, reconstructed in a monumental style, has recovered all its symbolic value. It is an immortal symbol of Catalan spirituality, and also an unviolated sign of Catalan identity and resistance to oppression. In modern times Montserrat and her black Virgin have not lost anything of their attraction to believers and to tourists from all over the world. When the famous children's choir of Montserrat sings:

> Rosa d'abril, morena de la serra,
> de Montserrat estel,
> il·lumineu la catalana terra.
> guieu-nos cap al cel...

the heart of every Catalan is moved.

Above: Montserrat, the cloister of the abbot Argerich (18th century) in front of the basilica.
Below: Kissing of the Virgin of Montserrat.
To the right: The Virgin of Montserrat, "the Brownie", Virgin from the 12th century approximately. Object of Catalan, and universal, veneration.

Barcelona

Barcelona is a world in itself. A maritime capital, with one of the largest ports in the Mediterranean; an industrial capital, which attracted the demographic surpluses of the agrarian areas of all Catalonia and of the south of Spain; a symbolic and sentimental capital of the Catalan reality, in which the language has played a unifying and resistant role. It is an artistic and intellectual capital, and the initiator of the great currents on which Catalonia feeds. Barcelona is not one city but many. There is the over-populated and noisy Barcelona of the historical centre, the bourgeois Barcelona of the Eixample, the residential and sophisticated Barcelona of the Diagonal, Bonanova, Sant Gervasi or Sarrià, the Barcelona of fun of Montjuïc and Tibidabo... and a lot more.
The whole city looks towards the sea. It is towards the sea that the big avenues go, it is from the sea that Barcelona has developed in concentric waves towards the hills which surround it to the north and south.

Above: The port of Barcelona.
To the right: El Portal de la Pau (The gate of peace) with the monument of Christopher Columbus and the customs building.

Roman and Gothic Barcelona

The history of Barcelona started on the little hill, situated in the middle of the bay, which the medieval documents call Mount Taber.

The territory was occupied originally by the Iberian tribe of the Laietans. The Carthaginians gave it the name of Barcino (from Barça, name of the ruling family of Carthago). After being conquered by Cornelius-Scipio in 133 B.C. Barcelona became a Roman colony under the name of the Colony of Faventia Julia Augusta Pia Barcino and was integrated into Hispania Citerior, whose capital was Tarraco, now Tarragona.

The excavations of the last years have revealed two or three meters below ground the foundations of houses and remains of the narrow curved streets, which still provide the basic network for the Gothic Quarter, and a perfectly organized drainage system. The columns of the temple of Augustus were salvaged and part of the Roman walls, miraculously saved from destruction because of the houses which had been built against them over the years, has been restored. After the fall of the Roman Empire Barcelona became visigothic and the king Ataulf made it the capital of an empire which stretched from Gaul to Hispania. The Arabs occupied it for nearly a century until the conquest by the Frankish king, Louis the Pious. From then onwards the fate of Barcelona was decided. The closest section of the Frankish Empire to the Muslems became a hereditary possession with Wilfred the Hairy, and thus began

the long dynasty of the counts of Barcelona, who became later the kings of Catalonia and Aragon. This dynasty made Barcelona into the queen of the Mediterranean, which was named "the Catalan lake".

The end of the 13th century and all of the 14th form the golden age of Catalan culture. It was at that time that all the great Gothic churches of the city were built, the cathedral, Santa Maria del Mar, the monastery of Pedralbes, as well as the

Above, to the left: The Royal palace (13th - 16th century) with the tower of king Martí.
Above: "Modern" façade of the cathedral made according to the plans of 1408.
To the right: The cathedral's façade reflected in the windows of a modern building in the Plaça Nova.

124

most beautiful civil buildings of the
Gothic Quarter, the Palau Reial Major,
the Palau of the Generalitat and the
aristocratic houses of the great families of
Barcelona. With a few exceptions the
Gothic Quarter archieved the same
physionomy as it possesses today. The
Palau Reial and the Cathedral form
a magnificent architectonic line of towers
and spires which dominate the old city.
Built apparently on top of the Praetorium
of the Roman colony, the Palau Reial was
for many centuries the residence of the
count-kings who enriched and enlarged it
as they grew wealthy. Restored after 1936
it has been the site of different museums
representing Barcelona's history. The
Gothic cathedral was built on the spot of
the old romanesque cathedral of
Berenguer the elder. Its façade and
modern spire, made from plans of
a French architect of Rouen in 1408, give
it a very French touch. The inside, with its
three vaulted naves and pointed arches is
totally Catalan; its cloister, in which the
gothic forms of the galleries and the old
trees figure exuberantly, is one of the most
lovely corners of the city. Every year
during Corpus week they make an egg
dance on top of the water fountain, "l'ou
com balla". It is a popular event with
children.
As well as its prestigious churches,
Barcelona has preserved from its gothic
golden age a lot of monuments of first
quality like the Llotja (stock exchange)
and the Drassanes (shipyard). Although
in all the big cities of the Catalan-Aragon

Above, to the left: Patio of the Palace of the
Marquis of Llió, in Montcada street, today
museum of clothes.
Above, to the right: exterior of the cloister
of the cathedral seen from Sant Sever street.
To the side: Angle of Assaonadors street
(Tonners street) and of the Plaça de
Marcús.
To the right: The Plaça de la Llana (wool
square).

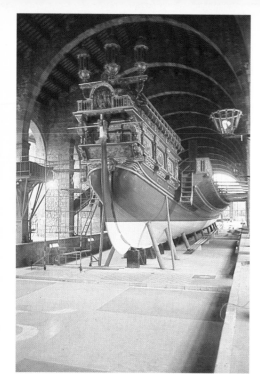

Confederation, like Perpignan, Tortosa, Valencia, Mallorca, Zaragoza and Barcelona, we find beautiful examples of Chambers of Commerce, only in Barcelona do we find still intact the Drassanes of the Middle Ages. The Drassanes, begun by Peter the Great and finished at the end of the 14th century by Peter the Ceremonious, is a magnificent building of various naves sustained by a diafragm of arches.

Situated at the bottom of the Rambla facing the sea it is unique in the world. There they built the great ships and Catalan merchant vessels which sailed the Mediterranean as far as the East from the 13th to the 14th century. The Drassanes have been converted today, very naturally, into the Museum of the Sea. Its rich collections of plans, old maps, promises to saints, naval and civil vessels tell us all the history of the maritime Catalonia.

Until the 13th century Barcelona remained inside the walls of the 4th century, but this square area was too small for the growing town. Further away from its fortifications, along the roads which led to its gates, there began to develop a whole net of urban nuclei like Sant Pere and Santa Maria del Mar, the first suburbs of Barcelona, and which James I, the Conqueror, encircled with a second wall in the 13th century.

Between the 13th century and 16th the life of the town shifted towards the maritime and commercial quarters like Santa Maria del Mar and la Boria, situated on the way to the beach.

Between these quarters there was

Montcada street, the width and straightness of which contrasted with the sinuous and narrow streets of the Gothic Quarter. In the sumptious palaces lived the enriched bourgeoisie and the nobles of Barcelona. When in the 18th century the centre moved towards the church of the Mercè and the Carrer Ample (wide street), the area of Santa Maria del Mar was slowly abandoned by the nobles and their palaces became artisanal and industrial dwellings.

Nothing was changed there from the 14th

Above, to the left: Exact reproduction of the galley of John of Austria, victor of the battle of Lepanto.
Above: Les Dressanes (Shipyard) today a Maritime Museum. The Capmany room dedicated to the Catalan fleet of the 19th century.
To the right: Nave of Santa Maria del Mar (14th century), the most important work of the Catalan gothic.

century. And although the palaces, until not long ago, were in ruin, their essential medieval architectural features had been preserved and could be restored. Separated from the Gothic quarter by the "Haussmanian" Via Layetana, the quarter of Santa María del Mar, like the rest of the old quarters of Barcelona, displays today a mixture of misery and splendour: misery of the over-populated and abandoned streets, splendour of the palaces of Montcada street and of the gothic elegance of Santa Maria del Mar.

Each gate of Montcada street opens on marvels: Palau Cervelló, Palau Dalmases, Palau de Castellet, Palau del marquès de Lliò, Palau Aguilar...
The municipality of Barcelona and private institutions have given a new vocation to a lot of these houses: the Palau Dalmases houses the Institute of Catalan Studies; that of the marquis de Lliò the surprising Rocamora collection of old dresses and the Palau Castellet and of Aguilar house the Picasso Museum. A visit to this street is essential to understand the evolution of

the monumental works of this painter. We find there the works of his Barcelona period, the series of the *Meninas* presented by the artist in 1968, and about one thousand works of his youth painted between 1897 and 1917. There are also famous pictures like "Las Manolas" from the cubist period or the Harlequin.
At the bottom of the silver-smiths street, or Argenteria street, an ancient path to the sea, you can see the silhouette of the octagonal spires of the church of Santa Maria del Mar. Built by James I at the

130

*Palau Berenguer d'Aguilar (14th C.)
today the Picasso Museum.
Above, to the left: The patio seen from the
gallery of the first floor.
To the right: The patio.
To the side: A room of the museum.*

time of the great Mediterranean conquests of the house of Barcelona, Santa Maria became the centre of the new capital of an empire of merchants and shipbuilders. The church is the purest example of Catalan Gothic. And its grace comes from the perfect equilibrium of its dimensions and the sobriety of its forms.

The Sardana

Danced everywhere from the most modest village square to big cities, the sardana is the national dance. Who knows if it came from Crete or Greek circle dances? The sardana is a dance of space, a circle of time, a cosmic symbol, an image of solidarity and a representation of life all at the same time. Despite the passing of time and changing of fashions, the sardana has not become "folklorized" like other popular dances. The regular rhythm, the succession of steps, the precise shrill of the instruments provide the framework which everyone follows. It is an act which is at the same time serious and gay.

The sardana is also the demonstration of an identity and in difficult times the Catalans have found in the sardana the manner for expressing a pacific resistance to oppression.

On Saturdays and Sundays, in front of the cathedral, the Barcelonese, old and young, poor and rich, enter into the circles.

The pleasures of the table

In winter in summer, day and night, in all areas of the city, one finds Barcelona sitting at the table.

The life of the cafés, cake shops and restaurants is essential. One starts the day in them by having a "tallat" (white coffee). One has lunch about three in the afternoon, which consists very often of little pre-cooked dishes of shellfish, prawns or fish, or various salads which you always find in the bars. Around 6 p.m. you can go to any cake shop, the favourite rendez-vous of high society ladies, and savour a cup of chocolate with cream, a dish of curds and honey, or one of those cakes much loved by Catalans. You can settle there comfortably, waiting for supper time.

There are the famous, or fashionable restaurants like the "Caracoles", frequented by international tourism, and where you see the photos of celebrities hanging from the walls: political, film, artistic, bull fighting or music-hall.

Others include the "Agut d'Avinyó", with some of the best cooking in Spain, the "Set Portes", an old renewed institution in what used to be a beautiful beer house and a lot more.

Some quarters specialize in certain foods — like the Barceloneta near the port where there is a line of restaurants along the shore, looking like barracks, and which serve fish and shellfish. The tourist

Above, to the left: A "cafe" of the quarter of the Pi; to the right: Restaurants of the Barceloneta.
Below: A sarsuela (fish stew).

lets himself be persuaded by employees of the restaurants who, in a few seconds, convince him in all languages that the restaurant of Señora Lola offers the best paella, the freshest gambas, or the best fish sarsuela.

All the shady little streets of the Born, the Gothic Quarter, the Pi and in front of the sea hide marvellous taverns, ideal territory for gastronomic adventures and where the atmosphere provides the first course.

This is the Barcelona which is loved by the tourists... as well as by the Barcelona people.

Modernism

For Catalonia the 18th century was
a black century during which its identity
was attacked by the enormous
centralizing efforts of the Bourbon
monarchy. Barcelona, still medieval,
dozed for almost two centuries, dreaming
of its imperial achievements.

Until about the middle of the 19th century
Barcelona was just a provincial citadel
where one hundred and fifty thousand
inhabitants lived enclosed behind the 13th
century walls. With the birth of industrial
society, accumulation of capital, the
opening up of national and international
markets by the Catalan bourgeoise and
the penetration of European ideas and
fashions, Barcelona revived after 1860 to
experience a new prodigious adventure.
While Spain, after the loss of its colonial
empire, was falling into a deep decadence,
Barcelona experienced a resurrection.
The Renaissance caused sleepy Catalonia
to develop a strong nationalism which
expressed itself by a linguistic renewal and
found its major outlets in poetry and
architecture. The starting point of this
renaissance was the commission given to
a Catalan engineer, Ildefons Cerdà, for

*Above: Passeig de Gràcia, the front of the
Casa Batlló (Gaudí).*
*To the right: La Casa Ametller (by Puig
i Cadafalch) and the Casa Batlló.*

a project of urban expansion for Barcelona (L'Eixample). At the end of the 19th century the city became a gigantic creation and was enlarged on the basis of a new American urbanistic pattern which broke definitively with the ties of the Middle Ages. The Catalan industrial aristocracy wanted above all to make a new city, which lacked nothing present in the existing models or in the tastes of the time. A really Catalan city. The Art Nouveau movement, known as Modernism here, appeared in Barcelona before anywhere else in Europe, and in the first years of the 20th century revealed the signs of a new Barcelona.

This fantastic creative explosion started to attract the curiousity of the European avant-garde: dadaists and surrealists, artists and writers turned their eyes to the Catalan capital and came there to experience the freshness of new inspirations.

Modernism, supported by a reborn population, and by the money of a bourgeoisie which wanted to reaffirm its refound strength, found its interpreters in Domènech i Montaner, Puig i Cadafalch,

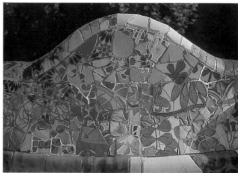

Parc Güell. Above: The dragon fountain.
Below: painted roof of a gate-house.

Abstract mosaics on the benches.
To the right: Gate-house of the park.

Gaudí and a whole new school of architects, graphic artists and artisans. Barcelona owes to them an impressive variety of monuments, houses, shops, urban furniture which have permanently determined its looks.

In the year 1908 the Palace of Catalan Music was inaugurated near the cathedral. The Palace designed by Domènech i Montaner, a structure of cement and steel supported by marble and mosaic columns, gigantic jewels, is a violent and almost sensual example of the new Catalan aesthetics.

At the same time in the Passeig de Gràcia was built the "Mançana de la discòrdia" (the block of discordance) named in this way because of the contrasts between its different buildings, with the Ametller house in the neo-gothic style by Puig i Cadafalch, the curious Batlló house, covered in mosaic by Antoni Gaudí. A bit further up in the same avenue, there is the Casa Milà by Gaudí with its ondulated façade and its lined up chimneys, in battle

order, which look like threatening warriors.

The Güell palace near the Chinese quarter, the Güell Park, and the Sagrada Família are the three major works of Gaudí.

The Modernist renaissance was dominated by the exceptional qualities of the greatest visionary of this century, Antoni Gaudí.

Heir of the whole Mediterranean civilization, from the Greeks to Michelangelo, including the Arabs, inspired by the Gothic richness of Barcelona and by the tortuous geology of his country, Gaudí, considered by some as the high priest of bad taste, was a non classifiable and universal genius who expressed himself in a naturalism which was at the same time exuberant and rational.

Architecture was for him the meeting point of all arts and techniques. To be able to express reality in its minutest details he became when necessary sculptor, wood

Sagrada Família.
Above: Shadow and detail of a tower.
To the right: The façade of the Passion,
finished recently.

worker, iron worker, ceramicist and painter and created a new architectonic language and was sustained by an almost mystical faith, by his Catalanism and by his obsession for work.

The Güell Park, an unfinished attempt to create an ideal city, the chapel of the Güell colony in Santa Coloma de Cervelló, the House Batlló, the Milà House and the Vicens House are his better known works but the one which gave him his universal fame was the Sagrada Família.

The silhouette of the four spires of the façade of the Birth are for the whole world the symbol of Barcelona, its Eiffel Tower, its Statue of Liberty. Gaudí devoted forty years of his life to it before he died, run over by a tram in 1926. The interrupted works were taken up again in 1940 and not long ago they finished the façade of the Passion. Perhaps it was better that the work had been left unfinished...

Above and to the right: Modernist style shops in the Rambla and the streets around.

142

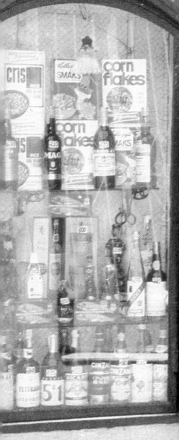

Fca de PASTAS ALIMENTICIAS

Tapiocas

The Plaça de Catalunya and the Rambla

Until about 1850 the people of Barcelona who wanted to escape from their medieval narrow streets and take the air outside the walls would come out through the Gate of the Blind and they would find themselves suddenly in an open field, traversed by a torrent. The better off had there small houses to spend Sundays or their holidays. Even though there was a real demographic explosion at the end of the 19th century, they had to wait a few years to realize the old project of making there a monumental square. They pulled down all the buildings and the Plaça de Catalunya became in a few years the lively nucleus of the new Barcelona, the scene for anger or happiness. Around its fountains, its gardens and its colourful pavement the cinemas, the smart hotels, big stores, travel agencies, restaurants, and fashionable shops are grouped. The big national and international banks have

Above and to the right: La Plaça de Catalunya in the evening.
Below: The Rambla at night.

144

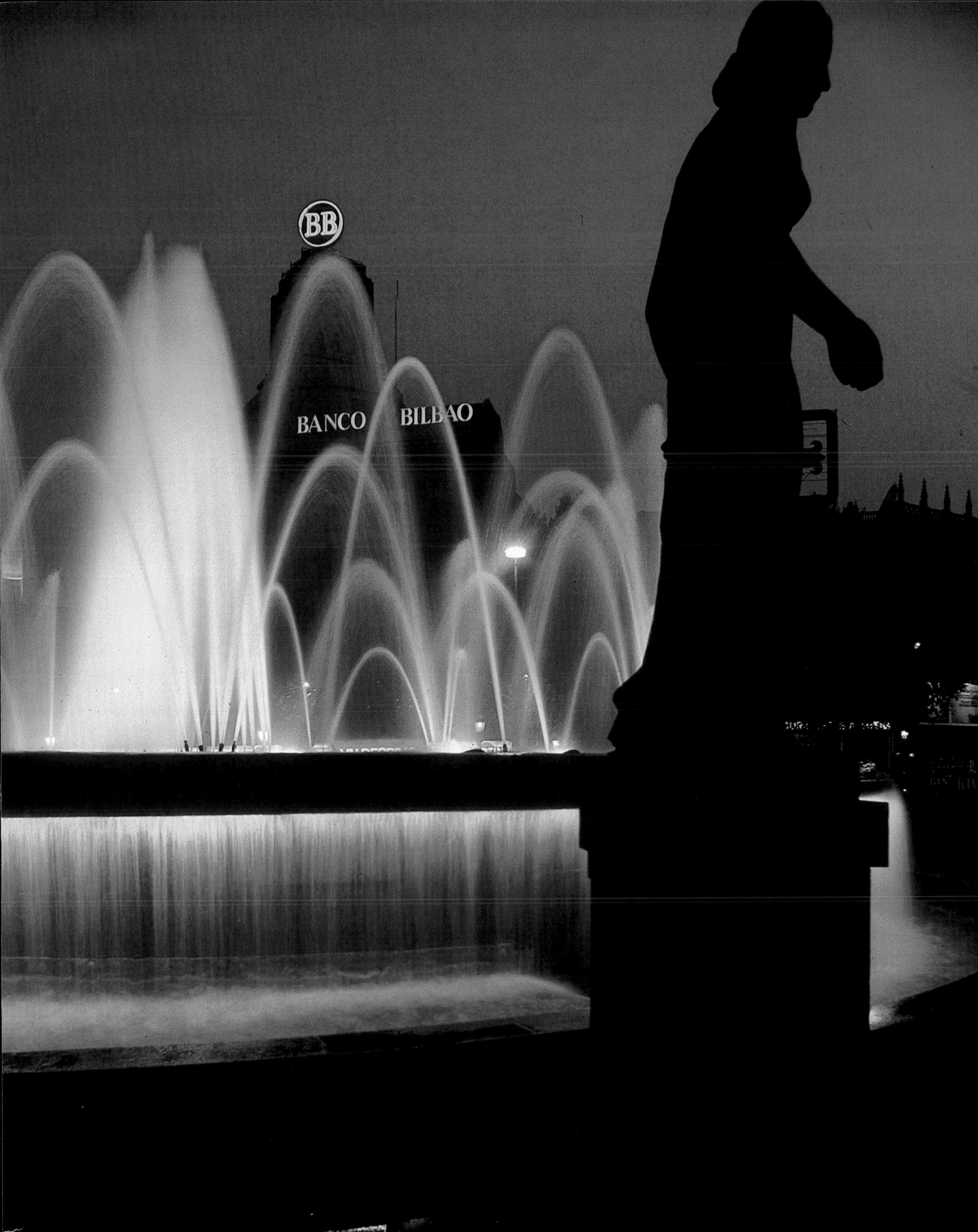
BB
BANCO BILBAO

their offices there as well. The Plaça de
Catalunya is a lake constantly filled by
traffic from the big avenues of the city, the
Granvia, the Rambla de Catalunya, the
Passeig de Gràcia and particularly the
Rambla towards the port. For more than
a hundred years the Rambla has been the
soul of Barcelona. Originally the Rambla
was the bed of a torrent which went
towards the sea and passed the base of the
fortifications built in the 13th century by
Jaume I. It was the limit of the west side of
the city. Like the esplanade which became
the Plaça de Catalunya, the Rambla and
the lanes leading off it were frequented by
the Barcelona people. It was already
a place of reunion and trading. There,
were the stands for selling meat, the
corrals for the herds of sheep, the straw
was weighed there... and also criminals
hanged.
Between the 16th and 17th centuries the
eastern side of the Rambla was occupied
by religious congregations: Jesuits,
Carmelites, Augustinians and Franciscans

*Above and to the right: The Rambla, the
Boqueria or market of Saint Joseph.*

built there their convents and schools. The convents on one side, the walls on the other: you have there the appearance of the Rambla until the end of the 18th century. The pulling down of the walls in the 19th century, the progressive disappearence of the convents, the planting of plane trees from the Devesa of Girona, the construction of blocks of houses, the opening of squares and adjacent streets, gave it slowly its present aspect. For the ignorant foreigner the Rambla appears as a uniform boulevard about one and a half kilometers long, from the Plaça de Catalunya to the sea, without interruption. Certainly the Rambla is always in all seasons the place of reunion and the permanent promenade area for Barcelonese people, foreigners and strangers, a real human current which groups together a world of the most varied origins. Still if you look carefully you will see that the Rambla can be divided into five different parts, each with its own life, its own specialities and its own rhythm. At the top, next to the gates of the new Barcelona, and next to the metro entrance, there is Canaletas, the traditional meeting place of all football fanatics. They meet in small groups to talk about the last game of "Barça", the Barcelona club.

The Rambla dels Estudis is where a university used to be and which Philip V transformed into a garrison to eliminate the dangers of subversion. Today it is the bird market. The writers have re-baptized it: they call it "the Rambla dels ocells" (the birds Rambla) because of the thousands of sparrows which live in the plane trees.

After the birds come the flowers. The Rambla de les Flors which for a long time was the only place in Barcelona where you could buy flowers in beautiful stands. This becomes a colourful garden which offers itself to painters and photographers. It provides the universal postcard of Barcelona. Next to it, a bit self-conscious with its metallic structure, the market of Saint Joseph exhibits the opulence of its

La Plaça Reial (19th C.). The lamp is a work of Gaudí's youth.

149

stalls of fruit, vegetables, poultry and fish artistically arranged. The Rambla of the Caputxins is the point where two worlds meet: that of the Barcelona bourgeoisie, who have there their most famous lyric temple, the Gran Teatre del Liceu, and that of the misery of the Chinese quarter. As the Rambla approaches the sea it seems to shake off its good manners and the correction which until now it has shown. Here in the Rambla de Santa Mònica, Barcelona takes on the

cosmopolitan and disorganized air of all the big ports. It is the nocturnal world of the illusionary adventure, of romances which have a price and of dim lights. On the terrace of the "Cosmos" you can spend hours observing the never ending movement of prostitutes, transvestites, of pimps, of the immigrants from the south, of pedlars, beggars and tourists and when the American fleet stops here the ambiance of the Rambla de Santa Mònica and the near streets suddenly improves in

tone: it is the time for noisy orgies and the easy dollar.

Inside the old city, on the site of the old Caputxin convent, like an open, romantic patio, the Plaça Reial, with its arcades and ochre façades built in the 19th century in neo-classical style, gives Barcelona a slightly Italian air. The benches, the bars and cafés are today the refuge of all the marginated. The Rambla is the shop window of Barcelona and the résumé of its magic. You can register there the city's

Above, to the left: One of the last carriages of Barcelona; to the right: The secondary activities of the Rambla and of the Portal de la Pau.
Below: Children in the park of the Ciutadella.

political, artistic, sportive or social pulse. You can watch or be watched, talk or listen. It is also the place of the lonely dreams and sometimes of the hopes of a whole people. Until not very long ago Barcelona people felt it almost a duty to have a daily walk down the Rambla.

Autonomous Catalonia

On the 25th of October 1979, the Basque country and Catalonia received their statutes granting autonomy. During the long Franco period the Catalans knew how to preserve what is for them the base of everything: their language. Politically they came out of the dictatorship very broken but the language stayed alive, strong for the new fight. They had had autonomy and a statute twice previously this century. From 1914 to 1924 the Mancomunitat of the four Catalan provinces had been a first experience, though closer to administrative decentralization than to a real autonomy. Primo de Rivera suppressed it.

In 1931 Barcelona was one of the first cities in Spain to show enthusiasm for the Republic and Catalonia voted strongly for its own autonomy. Eighty per cent of Catalans voted and 90 % were in favour. This time autonomy meant something: Catalan became the official language in conjunction with Castilian: the Generalitat with its president, an executive council and the Parliament obtained important administrative, judicial and police powers. This second experience left behind the bitter taste of internal fights, of broken hopes and of the disintegration during the Franco period. But it left intact the feeling of individuality the vivaciousness of the language and the obstinate dynamism. On the 11th of September 1977, for the first time since

the Civil War, Catalonia celebrated amidst general rejoicing its national festivity, the "Diada", which commemorates the resistance of the Catalans to the troops of Philip V on the 11th September 1714.

This real joy we have re-encountered at all the major demonstrations that during two years have prepared for the October referendum of 1979. "We want the Statute" was the cry.

Demonstration for Catalan autonomy in April 1979. Plaça de Tetuan and Passeig de Sant Joan.

Demonstration for autonomy in 1979.
Parc de la Ciutadella.

Montjuïc and Tibidabo

Montjuïc ("Mont Jovis", the mountain of Jupiter) and Tibidabo are the two places with a view in Barcelona. The 540 meters of altitude of Tibidabo make it the ideal observation spot to understand the urbanistic evolution of the city and to measure the incredible, present explosion of the suburban areas. Like all the big modern megalopolises, Barcelona appears as the victim of a growth too sudden to have avoided the chaos, the ruptures and the uniform ugliness of quick building at cheap prices. Tibidabo and Montjuïc, converted at the beginning of the century into parks, and protected by the urban plans, have fortunately been saved from this savage development. The slopes of Tibidabo are still covered by pine woods and a pleasure fair has been built at the summit.

On Montjuïc the municipality maintains magnificent gardens but it serves particularly as the acropolis for the conservation of culture and Catalan art. The Poble Espanyol, remaining from the International Exhibition of 1929, contains the traditional architectonic caracteristics of all regions of Spain. The Museu d'Art de Catalunya is one of the richest in the world on account of its collection of Catalan medieval art. It is also in Montjuïc that you find the Joan Miró Foundation. The architecture of Josep Lluís Sert serves to show off amazingly well the works of this other great Catalan artist.

Above and to the side: Montjuïc, Fundació Joan Miró.
To the right: Barcelona seen from mount Tibidabo.

Sitges

Sitges is to Barcelona what Deauville is to Paris or Brighton to London with the difference that Sitges is only 35 kms. away from Barcelona.

But the proximity alone does not account for the international prestige of this fashionable beach. There was something else needed to attract hither both the bourgeosie of Barcelona and also a sophisticated cosmopolitan crowd since the beginning of this century. Sitges is a minor, hilly outcrop before you reach the big monotonous beaches of the Tarragona coastline. That is its secret. The pointed end of Sitges enters into the sea like a spear between the beaches. It was here that were situated an old castle and a parochial church of rose colour. The charming church of la Mare de Déu del Vinyet is erected at the far end of the old village and is white like a marvellous graphic complement, a tail for a wedding dress. Other mediterranean villages have had the privilege of such visual charm but very few have preserved it. Amongst all the disasters of the touristic cataclysm which have destroyed everything on the coast in Catalonia and much further to the south, Sitges appears like a miracle. Even though for the last eighty years everyone has been fighting to own a tiny bit of land on the golden beach, and although they have built a lot, Sitges still preserves the elegance of its maritime promenade, the eternal grace of its old narrow and steep streets, and the interest of its three museums. But Sitges has also a great will power.

A lot is needed to resist eighty years of popularity without losing authenticity. It

Sitges, the Passeig Marítim.
To the left: the church of Sitges seen from the Platja d' Or.

is a surprising fact that Sitges succeeds in being both a very traditional Catalan village and the permanent fashion spot. From Spring to Autumn Sitges is the scenario for a lot of festivals and cultural demonstrations which attract "all" Barcelona and artists from all over Europe.

The local people have got used to the eccentricities which form part of the folklore of the village and contribute to its success. Apart from the festival of Sant Bartomeu, which is one of the most typical of all Catalonia, with its "moixiganga", a solemn and baroque dance, the big day of Sitges is in April, Corpus Christi. Its coincidence with the exhibition of carnations has perpetuated the custom of covering all the streets of the old village with a carpet of flowers. Each street makes its own design and the best is given a prize by a jury. After having been admired by the tourists all day long, in the evening the procession of Corpus, and the giants which follow the procession, walk on top of these ephemeral works of art. This is the beautiful way in which Sitges celebrates Spring.

Above and to the right: Sitges, carpets of flowers on Corpus day.

Tarragona

Tarragona is the ecclesiastical capital of our country but now there is no cardinal. He is in Barcelona. Everything is in Barcelona of course. I have known Tarragona when they said it was a dead city. It was lovely. The Rambla which is often empty is like the balcony of the Mediterranean and there is the archaelogical walk which starts there, the Roman architecture, the Roman ruins and of course the cathedral with the museum next to it and the palace. It was an adorable world with unforgettable friends. And there was still the Serrallo area, with some restaurants which cooked good fish at decent prices. It was a city to stay in, and it seemed that everything was better there. There was the fishermen's port and the commercial one. One of the most amusing things then in the area were the arguments between the people of Reus and those of Tarragona. The ones of Reus considered themselves superior and they were, the ones of Tarragona considered themselves more normal and this, too, was what they were. And so the time passed agreeably like that. I have never known if the phrase, "Reus, Paris and London" was a local invention or if it came from somewhere else.

Gate of Tarragona cathedral, statues of the apostles (13th and 14th C's).

The great phenomenon of Tarragona has been produced these last few years: it is the industrialization of the south part of the city. They have made a considerable port of petroleum, an oil refinery and a lot of large foreign and national companies have been attracted. Today the city is different. Salou and Cambrils are at the same time the most touristic centres on the coast. All this movement has produced a lot of life. That is certain.

A constant puzzle: the countryside of Tarragona is very well cultivated. Generally speaking the Tarragona land is arid. The question is why don't they irrigate this land with all the large amount of water that the Ebre pours into the sea? There are two valid arguments for doing this:
firstly to irrigate as far as possible the land of Tarragona would lead to a great increase in local resources. And secondly the completing of this project would provide Barcelona with a great quantity of water and Barcelona has the worst drinking water on this continent. Anyway all those who at some stage have passed through Amposta have been able to see the

quantity of water from the Ebre lost in the sea. They have even said that this project could be realized without using the waters of the Ebre but with the water the Ebre collects from the Segre which is the principal Leridan tributary and thus Catalan. Anyway this project should be studied with a more positive interest and equanimity.

Good news for the country and Tarragona: the whole of the restoration of Poblet is nearly finished. That is very good news. Thank you very much.

Poblet was scandalously destroyed the year 35 of the last century (the abolition of mortmain by the Mendizábal ministry) mainly for purposes of robbery. The destruction was total and lasted a long time. Today we know a lot about it thanks to the book of Eduard Toda which is essential. The destroyers of course had no problems in damaging the works of art, and they thought that in the tombs of the Catalan kings they would find gold. They didn't find a single ounce. Later two young Reus people became very enthusiastic about Poblet. They were the architect Gaudí of the Sagrada Família and Sr. Toda, in the diplomatic service, who served with great distinction in the most remote places of the world. Afterwards he bought Escornalbou which he filled with books which he gave later to Barcelona libraries. I have seen Escornalbou and met Sr. Toda personally. He was one of the great intellectuals of this country in the last years of the last century and at the beginning of this one. His passion for Poblet and his initial liberalism gave him an erroneous idea. He thought that Poblet had to be restored thinking only of the architecture and aesthetics. The Cistercian order opposed this and Poblet came back to life when the monks arrived from Italy and Croatia. The restoration of the great monastery has been the work of the Catalan bourgeoisie, the State and of touristic interest, which brings about 100.000 visitors a year now. Out of nothing they have created an extraordinary thing.

A long or short stay in this area of Tarragona of the New Catalonia is very agreeable. It is so peaceful. Valls, Montblanc, Prades in the mountain and Falset, El Vendrell, Salou, Cambrils, Torredembarra and a lot of other places and naturally Tarragona, Reus and Tortosa are very agreeable and interesting places. The small villages and landscapes are fascinating, they are so natural. Although we have talked a lot about the monastery of Poblet we should not forget the marvellous neighbouring monastery of Santes Creus, which has a more feminine and delicate grace.

J. P.

Street of Prades.

Vilafranca del Penedès, Museum of wine, Catalan ceramics.

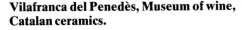

The wine country

To the left: Vilafranca del Penedès. Sign in worked iron. Museum of wine.
Above: Under the walls of Montblanc.
Below: Cellars of Raventós-Codorniu.

Between Barcelona and Tarragona a vast plain extends itself which is slightly inclined towards the beaches of the Golden Coast. The Penedès. No natural geographical feature tells us that we are passing from one province to the other. The Penedès is an immense vineyard which extends from the gates of Barcelona to the lands of Tarragona. From medieval times the wines produced have been high in alcohol content because of the strength of the sun. Table wines, sweet wines, liqueurs and wines for export for mixing with lighter wines have enriched the area and its capital, Vilafranca del Penedès, where a museum of wine, a real résumé of the social and economic history of the county, has been created in the old palace of the Catalan-Aragonese kings. Some of these wines are amongst the best in Spain but the best known are the ones around Sant Sadurní d'Anoia, champagne wines which are exported all over the world. The wine gives the region its character. The landscape, the everyday rhythm, the architecture of the villages and country houses, the festivals and social and economic relations have been for centuries, and still are, dictated by this enormous common effort which is involved in the tradition of wine-making. Towards the south the great mantle of the vine surrounds Poblet and Santes Creus where the two sister communities for centuries have looked after rich vineyards; it borders too the towered walls of the ducal village of Montblanc which has remained for centuries absolutely unchanged in a marvellous state of conservation and terminates at the entrance of Tarragona where the olive tree, the evergreen oak and the orange tree start to dispute the land.

Poblet and Santes Creus

If Ripoll was the birth place of Old Catalonia's reconquest and the tomb of its reigning counts, Poblet was the centre of Catalonian-Aragonese confederation and the chosen mausoleum of its kings. After having definitively thrown out the Moors and moved southwards the centre of gravity of Catalonia, Ramon Berenguer IV, count of Barcelona, wanted to express his gratitude to God by founding a new monastery. In 1149 he sent for monks from the Cistercian abbey of Fontfreda in Languedoc who built the monastery and started to work the lands of the community. For the kings of Aragon the monasteries of Poblet and Santes Creus were at the same time a pied-à-terre between Barcelona and Zaragoza, a royal shooting lodge and a place of retreat and sanctity.

Favoured by the kings, and enriched with donations, the two monasteries prospered until 1835 when their possessions were sold and the buildings were abandoned and pillaged. For a whole century there was nothing, just silence and desolation. These two abbeys were started in the middle of the 12th century, when romanesque art had reached maturity, and were finished in the gothic style. Later the tastes of different periods left other

Monastery of Poblet.
Above: Door of St. George's chapel of the 15th century.
To the right: Baroque door of the abbey and the buildings of the monastery.

emprints in the monasteries.
The masterpieces of Poblet and Santes
Creus are the church and the cloister.
They have all the sobriety and purity of
line of all Cistercian buildings. The naves
of the churches, with rounded vaults, the
sculptured stones and the leafy capitals of
the cloisters and fine columns of the
chapter houses as well as the vaults of the
dormitories illustrate the gentle passage
to Gothic art. The tombs of the kings,
richly sculptured, and from a later period,
show the Flemish influence.

Monastery of Santes Creus.
To the left: Cloister (14th C.) and fountain
for ablutions.
Above: Baroque gate of the monastery.

Tarragona

Like all old cities, Tarragona owes its origin to its strategic position. A hill in front of the sea, surrounded by rich land and situated at the meeting place of major communications networks. The hill of Tarragona has a glorious history. The Greek Polibi and the Roman Titus Livius refer to the settling on this spot of the tribe of Corsetans who made Corse their capital. In 218 B.C. the brothers Scipio, as soon as they had landed in Empúries to cut Hannibal's line of communications, occupied the hill which is protected by the first Iberian walls.

This is the way Roman colonization began and this was the origin of the extraordinary growth of Tarragona which the Scipios and their successors used as a base of operations for the conquest of the Peninsula. It is also through Tarragona that the language, the arts, the forms of life and the religion of the Roman conquerors was introduced, and which gave rise to a new civilization the

*Above: Tarragona, archaeological walk.
The old walls.
To the right: Roman aqueduct of les
Ferreres, arch of Berà, tower of the Scipios.
Below: Tarragona, cyclopic gate of the
archaeological walk.*

inheritance from which is still measurable.
Under the name of Tarraco the city
prospered during the Roman hegemony.
Caesar, who lived there for two years,
made in the provisional capital of the
Great Empire and his nephew Octavius
Augustus elevated it to the rank of capital
of Hispania Citerior. Considered if not
Rome's equal at least as its first daughter
it benefited from the same privileges as
the mother city. Augustus, Adrian and
Septimus Sever lived there. Like all
Roman cities Tarraco had a theatre,
baths, a forum, a praetorium, an
amphitheatre, temples and villas. It is
believed that it was Trajan who gave it the
aqueduct and the Arch of Berà. It was at
that time that the city was at its apogy and
had about thirty thousand inhabitants. It
must have looked like all the old cities of
the Mediterranean in which the mildness
of the climate, and the profits from an
intense commercial life, encouraged
peaceful development. Converted to
Christianity by St. Paul, the tradition has
it, it became the seat of the bishop, the
primate of Spain.
Its decadence though came from the north
with the Franks who besieged it in 264,

and the Visigoths who took it in 476. Of these black times we don't know much, nor do we know much more about what happened after the disasters caused by the Arabs in the 7th century. For about four centuries life fled from the hill of the first Hispanic capital and there were only ruins left. Tarragona did not become occidental and Catalan until after the reconquest of the south territories by Ramon Berenguer III who gave the city to the bishop of Barcelona. A new city dominated by the cathedral was built on top of the ruins of the preceding one. Between the Middle Ages and the 19th century it acquired a university and a new port and rose to the rank of provincial capital. In 1813 the troops of Napoleon occasioned disasters but without stopping its growth. Around Tarragona, the Arch of Berà, the tower of the Scipios, the mausoleum of Centcelles and the aqueduct of the Ferreres are the best preserved Roman monuments.

The most impressive inheritance though is the one we discover along the archaeological walk along the impressive remains of the old walls. The origin of these cyclopean blocks is not definitely known. For a along time it has been thought they were Tuscan, Iberian, Greek or Carthaginian. They formed the base to the successive walls of Tarragona and each conquest has contributed a strata like a geographical formation. Apart from the archaeological walk, embellished today with flowers and cypresses, you can also read the past of the old Tarraco in the ruins of the amphitheatre built next to the

Above, to the left: Tarragona, gothic patio of the Casa Castellarnau, today the municipal museum; to the right: Street of the cathedral area.
To the side: Entry to a bourgeois house of the Ramblas.
To the right: Tarragona, cloister of the cathedral.

sea, and in the palaeochristian necropolis and in the rich collections held in the Archaeological Museum. The cathedral is medieval. Apart from the fortified tower which is late Romanesque, the building is in the ogival gothic style with later al ditions showing Flemish, plateresque and baroque influences. The cloister, one of the most beautiful of Catalonia, is surprising because of its size.

Tarragona is, though, more than a museum city enclosed within millennary walls. It is a bourgeois town with its Rambla and its balcony over the Mediterranean; it is a working class town with the Serrallo, the fishermen's area, where in bars and restaurants they serve the whole range of sea products, accompanied by the "romesco" sauce. It is an industrial city with its oil-refining zone, and a touristic town as well, being the geographical centre for the big migrations to the Costa Dorada. Tortosa, a big agricultural centre, dominated by its Gothic cathedral, which resembles that of Barcelona, is the southern sentinel of Catalonia and has acquired its own character with its Aragonese, Valencian and Catalan mixture.

It is here that the Ebre marks the boundary of the New Catalonia. On the south side of this river the Valencian region can be perceived.

Above: Rice field of the delta of the Ebro. To the left: The delta of the Ebro, wide and lonely, is a paradise for shooting and fishing. (Photos: Raimon Camprubí)

The author, Christian Sarramon, acknowleges with gratitude the collaboration, advise and ideas of:

Inès

Monsieur and Madame de Bordas

Señor Bosch-Corominas

Dominique Delavergne

Casa Díaz-Costa de la Bisbal

Patrick Duruy

Cristina Gasau

Christophe and Claude Jonquères d'Oriola

Enric Munné

Charles Noettinger

Teresa Ricart-Prohías

Louis-Charles and Martine de Roquette-Buisson

Didier and Anne Roques

Guim and Odile Rubert

Henri and Jacqueline Sarramon

Marie Claire Stengler

Teresa Xiquoira «Can Bernat»

Air Inter Airlines

Iberia Airlines

and all the voluntary and involuntary
actors in this book.

The design has been done by
«Editorial»,
and the map of Catalonia drawn by
France de Ranchin.

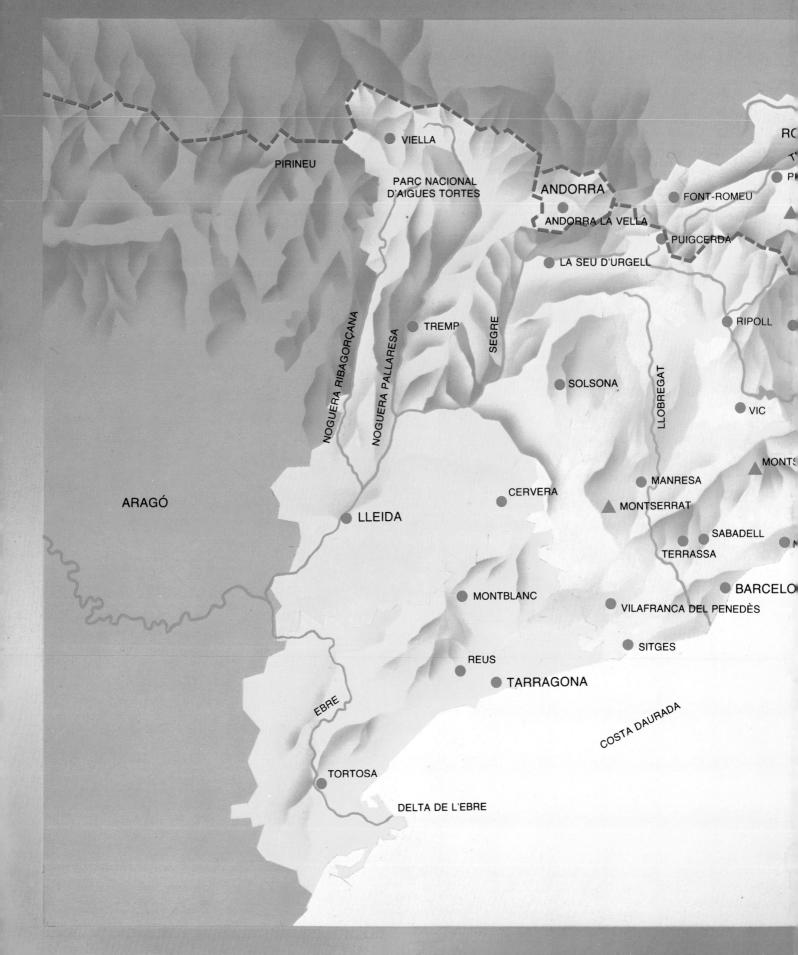

PIRINEU

VIELLA

PARC NACIONAL
D'AIGÜES TORTES

ANDORRA

ANDORRA LA VELLA

FONT-ROMEU

RO

T

PI

PUIGCERDÀ

LA SEU D'URGELL

NOGUERA RIBAGORÇANA

NOGUERA PALLARESA

TREMP

SEGRE

RIPOLL

SOLSONA

LLOBREGAT

VIC

ARAGÓ

CERVERA

MANRESA

MONTS

LLEIDA

MONTSERRAT

SABADELL

TERRASSA

M

BARCELO

MONTBLANC

VILAFRANCA DEL PENEDÈS

SITGES

REUS

TARRAGONA

EBRE

COSTA DAURADA

TORTOSA

DELTA DE L'EBRE